N..,

Crazy Brain

An Attempt to Cope with Multiple Sclerosis

Sylvia Wright's

(Clever?) Thoughts,
Jokes, Quizzes, Riddles
& Poems.

.

Copyrights

Text: © Sylvia Wright 2022
Cover & Graphics: © Cybermouse Books 2022
Cover Image   © Sylvia Wright 2022
Back Cover   © Bill Allerton (Sylvie's Back Garden!)
Typeset & Layout: © Cybermouse Books 2022
Font: Multiple Fonts

ISBN: 978-1-3999-2281-4

First published by Sylvia Wright 2022

In the design of this book, Sylvia Wright has made every effort to avoid infringement of any established copyright.

If anyone has valid concern re any unintended infringement please contact us first at the above address.

Jokes borrowed by Isaac Can-Spell from www.parade.com/jokes

I'm dedicating this book to my Mother
As she produced me and my brother,
To the memory of my Dad,
He had a good life, so don't be sad,

To my Sweetheart Steve,
It really upsets me that he did leave,
And to my son Marcus,
Just because.

The poet is a liar who always speaks the truth.

Jean Cocteau
1889–1963

The most completely wasted of all days is that
in which we have not laughed.

Nicolas Chamfort
1741–1794

Foreword

When I met Sylvia Wright we were both hanging around in a hospital corridor. I was waiting for my partner, Bryony, and Sylvia was doing what Sylvia seems to spend a lot of time doing. That 'doing' comprises mostly of being 'seen to' by the NHS.

Sylvia was in her wheelchair and we struck up a conversation during which I unashamedly proposed that she listen to podcasts on my newly-published Urban Tiger Radio. In turn, Sylvia proposed that I visit her website and accept regular emails from her that included her thoughts and poems on the month past.

Sylvia won.

I don't know if she ever listened to anything of mine but she keeps popping emails in my inbox with great regularity. Sometimes the content of these emails makes me groan, but it always leaves me with a smile.

Over the last few years I have learned a lot about Sylvia and, in the laying out and typesetting of this book, I have come to learn there is so much more and I'm now feeling a little self-short-changed for not having explored the sense of the person behind the emails further.

I hope this effort is of some recompense to my already overburdened conscience.

In our email conversations, and through an intense study of this book, I have come to appreciate the strength that lies within Sylvia, and the way she seeks positivity where most of us would not even dare to look. There is hope in here, a palpable lack of a 'Why Me?' philosophy, and an unfailing ability to grasp at opportunity as it fleets by her limited window.

If you are looking for negativity from Sylvia or from her situation, you will not find it here. Nor will you find a person who sits and lets Life and Love fly past them like straws in the wind.

Miss them if you will, and be depleted by that.

Sylvia won't.

Bill Allerton

Introducing Me,
Sylvia Wright

I've had progressive multiple sclerosis (MS) since 1994. I was also born with two half-wombs and one kidney. I met my husband Steve in 1999 when he sold me a mobility scooter.

I didn't believe I could have children or carry to term, but in 2005 our son Marcus was born.

From 1998, I recovered in a major way. I took a leap of faith (literally!) by doing a tandem skydive and by changing my diet and attitude. This new positivity helped me battle MS for years. Despite this since about 2009 the MS has progressed, to the stage where I'm now severely disabled and need lots of care and help. Don't feel too sorry for me though, as I'm in a better position now, thanks to the NHS, than I was in 2012, when I weighed less than six stone and was on the way out.

To repeat, I'm in a better position now. This being despite:

1. Multiple operations, including the insertion of a baclofen pump (for pain relief), cutting my hamstrings to ease the pain of my muscle spasms and removing bladder stones.

2. Being hospitalised multiple times for septicaemia, sepsis (caused by kidney stones) and pneumonia. On top of all this I was rushed to hospital after overdosing on water – yes water – as I had a compulsion that meant I drank and drank.

3. Having to be brought back by the Crash Team in December 2018.

These events all sound pretty major but in many ways they pale into insignificance when compared to making it through my everyday life; everyday life that has got substantially harder over the years and much, much, worse since Steve passed away in August 2020 from non-Hodgkin lymphoma.

My everyday life consists of:

1. Making it through the night on my own, with only my own thoughts for company until my carers arrive in the morning; the exact time of their arrival depends on the budget I have available.

Making it through the night isn't easy as I often don't sleep and have too much time to think negative thoughts in general, not just about losing Steve.

2. Once my carers arrive it is slightly easier but it's never really easy, my life is lived in my bed. The MS has

2

progressed so far now that I am unable to do anything for myself. Think about what that means – it means that carers do it all, they:

- · Clean me up each morning.
- · Shower me.
- · Brush my teeth.
- · Dress and undress me
- · Cook for me and feed me.
- · Give me my medication.
- · Turn me, move me!
- · Hoist me into my wheelchair.
- · Programme my TV.
- · Move my limbs for physio.
- · Make phone calls for me, and…

· so much more, I have no dignity in life now, actually no life, without them.

3. Battling my mind and body in the day time, which means:

- · Coping with my compulsion to burp all the time.
- · Coping with my need to know how much of my water ration (the doctors have me on a water restriction) I have left for the day.
- · Coping when the TV and Alexa are turned off. When they're on, they occupy my brain and distract me from negative thinking. I can turn them off when people visit, even though I would often prefer not to.

• Coping with a need to check and recheck what has been programmed into the TV, this is on top of me forgetting what has already been programmed.

• Coping with leg and arm spasms that I can't control, and which are worse since my baclofen pump stopped working in July 2020. The spasms happen at night as well.

I know deep down that the compulsions and phobias listed are illogical but...

...I did try and put what I cope with daily in a poem but it just didn't work, maybe that will come in the future.

However, I manage to live, and despite MS and COVID-19;

• I am a mother to Marcus!

• I call my friends – I wish I could visit.

• I see my Mum.

• I compose poems.

• I have the final say on the updating of my website;

www.livingwithms.co.uk

I have the final say on how my life is run.

Nothing is easy but I still do it.

I've written this book because I'm a survivor.

I think I have an interesting brain and funny and crazy thoughts, which I hope everyone can enjoy.

The book is called *My Crazy Brain* because that is where it has come from: Sylvia's Crazy Brain! It's corny but ama(i)zing, sorry for the pun but that's this book, I like looking at words and changing the meaning of them. I think the book ranges from good to kind of a rubbish genius in a way, it can be clever sometimes!

I'm a member of Britain's Bed-bound Got Talent!

I also wanted to prove to myself, and to others, that I've not just vegetated and done nothing but that I have created something unique, especially with the poems.

So please go ahead and enjoy my riddles, puns, jokes, quizzes and the truth and fun of my poems. The poems will hopefully also tell you more about me as a person, my life and my ongoing battle with MS.

Contents

Part 1 – Poems

Part 2 – Riddles & Jokes

Enter and enjoy…

POEMS

Limits

(February 1995)

This was my first poem. I think it shows that I was thinking deeply and philosophically about things as I contemplated the onset of MS, which I knew I had, even though it was then still undiagnosed.

I think the most intriguing and beautiful thing about this poem is the way I've linked my self-challenging thoughts into a wider mosaic of intrigue to ponder on.

Part of the poem's beauty is that every person who reads it will interpret it in a different way and will ask different questions; it'll paint a different picture for everyone.

I doubt there is really an answer to this poem as it is so philosophical.

Limits

Eat nothing, make yourself sick,
Eat yourself silly, make yourself sick,
These are the Limits.

Learn nothing, know 'nothing',
But the more you learn, the more you 'know',
You 'know nothing',
These are the Extremes.

See everything, see nothing?
See nothing, see further?
What are the Boundaries?

Perfect health, a 'perfect' life,
No health, No life,
Or something beyond life?
These are the Questions!

A 'perfect' life....100% joy,
But where is joy without sorrow?
Or sorrow without joy?
This is my Paradox.

Where is light without darkness?
To see further, must one not stumble in the
darkness?
The full spectrum of beauty emerges,
through sunshine and rain.

Perfection is pure beauty,
But where is beauty without appreciation?
Every need is catered for.
So where is love without need?
And where is beauty without Love?

The Desk of Life

(Spring 1995)

This poem I love, it's the one I'm most proud of; to me it's my best one.

Why? Because it is the most me, the most entropic poem of them all, but it works. It's random things linked together, just as my life is random actions linked together, and how my random thoughts link together.

I think it works well, much better than my life often has, it makes sense, well to me anyway, unlike life which often makes no sense at all. It brings meaning from the chaos. I was the entropic chaos when I wrote this; the poem is the genius that came from the chaos.

I hope I haven't over egged the build up to the poem and thereby taken away from its enjoyment; it's just that I believe you'll get as much pleasure from the poem as I do.

The Desk of Life

Calculator, Filofax, Ajax, duster,
Pile of books, discarded stockings,
Chewing gum, burnt toast.

The order in life is to live,
The 'disorder' in living is life,
Existence is ordering the disorder.

Order sharply and life becomes jagged corners,
Penetrating, harsh, cold and calculated...in a box,
One scrubs so hard... the friction burns,
Life is worn away.

Better to burn the toast, toast life,
... and digest the consequences.

Digestion requires the chewing of gum,
The hazard is choking,
Take too much and the risk is high,
The toast crumbles into dust... with no form.

The stockings of discarded innocence,
Used and abused... disintegrate into chaos,
... a random path... travelling far...
but leading nowhere!

The Ajax may not scrub it clean,
The files will always exist,
Get up! Dust yourself down!
Calculate the meaning in your head.
Express the thoughts with illustration.
Pile up the books.
LIVE & LEARN.

My Reality

(Summer 1996)

This poem is interesting as it philosophically and truthfully reflects transition and flux. The reasons for this transition and flux are manyfold, but a major trigger for it was that I had finally finished my university education and now needed to move on to something new.

So, I had many practical questions to ponder such as:
What should I do? What could I do? Could I do anything?
Could I live on my own, support myself, or did I have to go and live back with my parents?

I was also at this time facing the difficult choice of whether or not to get an official diagnosis of the condition that afflicted me, even though I knew that this might limit my options for the future. Facing a true reality, rather than faking one for myself, I had to lose my current path to find a new one, something very scary to do.

But it was not just that, although the whole foundation of my life was being challenged, that of my family and friends was too because they would have to face the beast of MS through me. Naturally, I was worried about how they would cope, how they would relate to me, whether they would want to relate to me or whether I was to become a leper in society.

This poem reflects all this, and more, of what was going on inside my head and, amazingly to me now, raises the question 'How can I help them face my MS?' I hadn't realised that I was such a tough nut in the face of MS, even back then.

15

My Reality

I live in my reality,
What I see, what I hear,
What I comprehend,
'My Reality'.

Change threatens my reality,
I am trapped by my comprehension,
I cannot comprehend,
I become lost.

I often break down,
In fear and confusion,
I become 'detached' from 'my reality',
but the 'act' goes on!

So, I must strive beyond,
Change my reality,
I must become lost to find myself,
I must lose myself to comprehension,
…to comprehend further,
…to grasp a new reality,
…to extend my limits.

But how to extend the limits of others,
who will never reach beyond a simple reality?
Their fear will remain…
…Only to be beaten by my Courage!

Lost Love

(July 1997)

What can I say about this poem? Apart from the fact that, in many ways, it was a mental scream, a release of intense emotions after one who I thought could have been the one to me, turned out not to be, as he stayed with the girl who I thought was his previous love.

I think this was a useful exercise as a poem, as it helped me to release emotion, but I think you will see from its tone and where it finishes, that it did not in itself resolve the issues and emotions the break-up had thrown up in me, as these are still being processed in the poem that follows this one, *Forsaken?*.

Looking at this poem now, and at *Forsaken?* too, it seems to me that these are poems that reflect me trying to find my place in the world, not just in relation to love, but also in relation to God and to the bastard syndrome that is MS.

Lost Love

You came to me a star so bright,
You lightened up my darkest night,
You gave me hope,
We shared such joy,
With you I'd cope,
Crazy I know.

I felt there was a plan to life,
A reason for the pain and strife,
I gave my all. I loved and lost,
Now yet again I pay the cost.

It was far too good to be true,
You came and went out of the blue,
My life's collapsed and you are gone,
And yet, somehow, I must strive on.

For Why? For What? I do not know,
There is no plan when life's so low,
All I wanted was a chance to love,
And help with God's great works above.

Yet my body is now trapping me,
What is the point? I do not see,
If I can't make the world a better place,
I'd rather leave but with God's grace.

In hospital I lay and ask God why?
He lets me cry and cry and cry?
What have I done that is so wrong?
I just want to float off and be gone.

Forsaken?
(Summer 1998)

This poem catches me at a very low ebb, there is nothing positive in it. It's not even asking the question 'Why me?', it's having a depressed grumble about my life, how I'd been left on my own with only the horror of MS for company.

At this time, MS was a real horror for me, you can see in the poem that I hadn't even started to come to terms with it, later poems show I did eventually, but I definitely hadn't at this stage.

No love, no one who understood, no belief in God, or at least great doubt in him, just me with MS on my tod, forsaken.

Forsaken?

Fatigue, numbness, paralysis,
Brain degeneration,
Praying for time,
Searching for someone,
Someone to be there,
Someone who'll love me,
Love the unlovable.

But all alleys are dead ends,
Men run away. It's only words,
Time always runs out,
No one can stop it,
No one can cope,
and I get what I dread,
Aloneness, emptiness, darkness.

I get torn into pieces,
No one understands,
They all have their 'Life Theories',
That I'm supposed to believe.

But they don't have this, do they?
THE RUTHLESSNESS OF MULTIPLE
SCLEROSIS!

MS Attack
(April 2000)

MS Attack is my first poem showing a change in my attitude towards MS and life. A change from feeling mainly negative about life and MS, to a generally more positive one in which I was fighting back on all fronts, fighting back to win. I say generally positive, because when facing anything as hard as MS we all have our moments of doubt about successfully overcoming it.

The amazing thing about this poem is the honest way in which I've dealt with the hardship and pain of MS, and the difficulty in finding the strength to face it.

It really amazes me now how I faced the hardship and found the positivity from somewhere inside of me, aided and abetted by my friends on and offline, to change from the negative person of 1998 to this combative lady who would surge back with the help and love of others from 1999/2000 on, and succeed as she refused to let MS control and defeat her.

The key thing about this poem and what I think makes it successful – if hard hitting – is that it came directly from the heart when I wrote it, not brain editing, just good old-fashioned honest, heartfelt truth.

MS Attack

MS makes its attack on me,
Whack after whack, oh where can I flee?
My body feels weak, my movements so slow,
I duck and I dive to avoid the next blow.

It beats me up. I'm black and blue,
Nine rounds with Mike Tyson,
How many more can I do?
My body is numb, I start to shake,
Please rescue me, I need a break!
But no one hears my desperate plea,
So I have to search inside of me.

I reach inside, what can I find?
A will to live and strength of mind,
I am so determined to survive,
To live my life, to Stay Alive.

So this torture I must withstand,
With faith, I'll find a helping hand,
Deep inside myself I find a strength,
To help me swim that extra length,
My stubbornness drives me from within,
To continue my search and Never Give In.

So I ride the storm. The skies WILL clear,
I KNOW that sunshine will appear,
And my sinking feet in the quick sand,
Will find themselves on solid ground,
and gingerly I'll get back on my feet,
For I will Never Accept Defeat!

My Leap of Faith
(Florida 2000)

This poem reflects the time when I had changed my life, after I had made the bravest decision in my life, to be honest to myself about me and MS.

It isn't about my skydive, even though that was part of my leap of faith because that was easy. It was deciding not to mope around and instead find and TRY things that would help me and put me on the right track in my fight against MS, that was the brave part.

This poem is great; it's inspiring as it shows the transformation from the depression of *Forsaken?* to the new Sylvie moving forward, facing her problems and looking to make the best out of life.

I love the optimism of it, how I had faced my fears, how they would not win I would out-stubborn them.

I'd made my decision, my leap and there was no going back. With my new love, Steve, and re-found faith at my back and a never ever give in attitude, I was going to have a really good shot at knocking out MS for good.

25

My Leap of Faith

I feel like stones being ground to dust,
My weary bones so full of rust,
I feel my life out of control,
Battering my torn and tattered soul,
Forcing me just like a slave,
Onward to an early grave.

But in truth this will not be,
For MS is not the enemy,
Like an anchor in the dock,
My faith holds firm. I am a ROCK,
Holding me where I belong,
Alive, Surviving, Steadfast and Strong.

I reject old patterns. I will not be told!
I accept all that happens and release the old,
My mind often yearns for that easy 'quick-fix',
But I must resist for it does not exist,
Only courage, faith and patience pays,
In reality, there are no easier ways.

I believe in success despite the MS,
The victim is gone, the more I strive on,
Through thick and through thin,
I WILL NEVER GIVE IN!
Despite all the strife,
I WILL LIVE MY LIFE!

I now have a formula I add to each day,My journey
to WELLNESS to keep MS at bay,
The pathway is stony. I stumble and fall,
And often I meet what feels like a brick wall.

But from this path I will not stray,
I BELIEVE there will always be a way,
To stop the progress of MS,
And transform the diagnosis to 'God Bless'.

So I ACCEPT all the tears
and release all my fears,
And I cling to the rope that signifies HOPE,
I know I will bleed but I know I'LL SUCCEED,
I'll believe in fate's plan and I'll pray all I can.

I will shine like a STAR for I have come so far,
A twinkling LIGHT
to help others with their plight,
MS may do its worst but my bubble won't burst,
WHACK AFTER WHACK, I KNOW I'LL BE
BACK!

I'll live my life, and laugh and learn,
For like a ROCK my faith is firm,
My goal is high to become fully well,
I reach for the sky! Only time will tell.

So I'll live for today, ENJOY THE RIDE!
The rest is for God to decide.
I now BELIEVE MS will set me free,
And truly be the making of Me!

Press Pause
(2001)

Dedicated to the memory of Ian White
(2nd May 1967–15th May 2001)

Press Pause reflects another change in my attitude to MS. The previous two poems, MS Attack and My Leap of Faith showed me, facing my future positively but with a slight devil-may-care attitude. What I mean by this is that I was intent on facing MS and getting on with life with no or little regard to the consequences of doing so.

By the time this poem was written, life had taught me that there can be a negative backlash if you disregard warnings and go forward hell for leather. Life had taught me that standing still, breathing and taking stock can be equally, if not more important, hence the name of the poem.

Press Pause, therefore, reflects an understanding that a positive pause, followed by a positive step, followed by more positive pauses and steps is actually a better, more sustainable, way forward to a better life than acting as if one were in the charge of the Light Brigade.

Having said all that, this poem is in many ways not just practical but also reflects a philosophical understanding of the above. I think it's important to recognise that 'Philosophical Sylvie' is back, as it reflects how far I had progressed by 2001, since the lows of the late 1990s.

Press Pause

Rich are the fruits of life,
Rich is the tapestry we weave.

My life is full and rich,
Many people connect with me,
They tell me their story,
People who need me, people who give to me,
People who teach and inspire me.

I live, I love, I journey on,
My Journey of Self-Discovery,
My life is my responsibility,
I create the life I want,
The formula is simple,
Thought, Action, Deed.

Life is rich but the core is basic,
Like the simple threads that weave our tapestry,
They come from within,
From stillness deep within the self,
From knowing the self,
From the power of being.

Yes, I am a doer,
But first and foremost a be-er,
Constant doing is not living,
Headless chickens!
Meaningless, chaotic and inefficient,
Leading to exhaustion and loss of the self,
Our lives flash by in an instant.

Ill-health surfaces, trying to slow us down,
Wakes us up, gives us time to think,
To breath, to rest our exhausted bodies,
And nourish our dying souls,
But too often only death can stop us,
Death is our only power.

Yet simply 'Being' presses 'Pause',
Being lets me breathe again,
Being gives me clarity and insight,
To do what really matters and do it well,
Being gives me strength and
calm through any storm,
Making anything possible,
I have the key within myself.

The picture is ever changing,
Life happens, life changes as the tide,
Up and down, to and fro,
I am but a student alert, aware and ready,
That is all that really matters,
Being gives detachment,
Simply 'Being' gives perspective.

So let not the tide sweep you under,
Let not death be your only shelter,
Look within yourself,
The 'Timeless Zone' is always there,
The still-point,
The point of nothing,
The point of everything,
The Self.

My Life Poem
(March 2016)

This poem describes the amazing life I've had and the amazing things I've done.

I wrote the poem to tell people what an amazing life I've led despite the onset of MS, and also to remind myself of the good times I've had and can have again. Writing it then and listening to it now definitely helps remind me that life isn't as bad as I sometimes think it is when I'm feeling down.

But there was more to writing the poem than that. I also wanted to present the real me, the good, the bad, the ugly of me, the randomness, the bizarreness, the entropic nature of me. In doing so, I wanted to challenge myself to stay that way and not to be overcome by boring habits that can pervade a slightly less-abled than average human's life.

It wasn't just about me, though, I also hope that what I present in the poem will challenge people to make the most of their lives while they have the opportunity; that they will take all the opportunities that come their way while still being true to themselves.

My Life Poem

When I was a teenager,
I was in serious period pain,
It made me yell out, and drove me insane,
I went to the Jessop Hospital; they found I had not
one womb but two,
Oh no, for babies that never would do,
Even worse. the blood from the left womb could
not get out,
Causing pain that made me scream and shout

After numerous surgeries,
the left womb had to be taken away,
For me, the day of that surgery,
was the very worst day,
As a woman I felt like I was no good,
Because I couldn't have a baby,
like a woman should,
Now I realise everyone deserves loving,
it's what they're worth,
And it's precious little to do,
with whether they can give birth.

I went on the pill non-stop,
to get through my GCSEs,
And I got the result of 8As and 2Bs,
At school me, Sara and Eleanor Waite,
Called each other, best mate,
Sara and I both fancied the chemistry teacher,
In our lesson plans,
chemistry therefore did feature,
Sara, like me, is as mad as a hatter,
And often at break we did chatter.

I sailed through my A Levels, then went off to
Sussex University,
Where I studied German and chemistry,
Sussex University is near Brighton,
Where the boys I did frighten,
Apart from Tom, Andy and Dave,
With whom I often did misbehave,
We were best friends and we surreally got on,
I really enjoyed hanging with Andy, Dave and Tom,
I worked hard and got a First, top marks,
I wish I'd believed in myself from the start.

MS started at 21,
Immediately I knew what was wrong,
This is because of a book I'd read,
A book that subsequently
would fill me with dread,
In the book, this vicar develops MS,
The author of the book signed it, God bless,
Multiple Sclerosis,

That I didn't want blessing with,
Who would have thought
I also had so much to give?
The book was a smile on the face of God,
I felt very alone, and on my tod.

I was diagnosed with MS after,
My immediate thought was 'Oh why me?'
In order to cope, I started smoking and drinking,
And my mind was full of negative thinking,

I smoked cannabis and drank wine,
To pretend to the world I was fine,
But MS was continuing to progress,
And I was feeling severely depressed,
I saw a wheelchair and it filled me with dread,
I said to my brother, 'Use that? I'd rather be dead.'

I hid my MS, told people I was drunk,
That shows how low I had sunk,
I think I was scared of friends running away,
But of course the best friends stay,
come what may.

When I did my skydive, I was all over the press,
I came out and told the world I had MS,
Old schoolteachers, school friends
and my family,
All went ahead and sponsored me,

I managed to raise over two grand,
Not bad for someone who could hardly stand,
I also met people I didn't know before,
They would become good friends I now adore.

One important contact was the Singleton family,
Stephen was the saxophonist from ABC,
Stephen started taking me out
to the swimming pool,
He was always larking about and playing the fool,
Then Sarah, his sister, wrote me a letter,
She advised: change your diet for the better,
I saw Brian Hampton, the great nutritionist,
Who told me what foods to eat,
and which foods to miss.

I followed my diet to the letter,
And within a month, started feeling better,
I was on a diet so strict, I diluted water,
It worked, my immune system
started behaving like it oughta,
Once a week on my hooray day,
With my strict diet, I could somewhat play,
I only broke diet, on that one day,
For more days than this I would heavily pay.

Through the skydive publicity,
I met Mr Steve Wright,
It wasn't love, more like laugh at first sight,
He sold me my mobility scooter,
that's how we met,
A moment in time we'll never forget.

He took me on holiday to the Sunshine State,
It was amazing in paradise, it felt like fate,
Steve had a house on Cudjoe Key,
Just the right size for him and me,
That's how we could go for so many weeks,
Steve and I fell in love;
it felt like it was for keeps,
The sunshine and swimming helped me recover,
I was happy in paradise, with my new lover,
We started to go for longer and
longer every year,
I was living my life and facing my fear,
My brother came to Florida
and on the sundeck was sat,
Steve was bashing coconuts and said,
'Do you want a coconut, Matt?'
After that the name 'Coco' just stuck,
And when Marcus was born, became Uncle
CoCoNut.

Steve wanted a webpage, so I learnt web design,
I built him a page,
and put the scooter business online,
The webpage took off
and we made plenty of money,
And I spent my life laughing
as Steve was so funny,
I made a deal with Steve on the webpage, regarding
commission,
I was so happy and busy working,
I found myself in remission,

I came off benefits, and became self-employed
When the webpage took off, I was overjoyed,
I did the webpage because I trusted my gut,
The webpage success was in part good luck,
I took the gamble on myself, yes I took the bet,
But they do say the harder you work,
the luckier you get.

I did his page by learning html,
Then I did one for me as well,
My MS webpage is www.livingwithms.co.uk,
On taking charge of MS, I had plenty to say,
The main topics were diet, nutrition,
swimming and sunshine,
These tools helped me reclaim life as mine,
I brainwashed my brain with positive thinking,
I faced my realities
and stopped smoking and drinking.

Steve not wanting kids was a big relief,
Because for me, kids could only mean grief,
I stabilised MS through putting myself first,
So with a baby, I could only see
MS getting worse,
I stabilised through good sleep
and avoiding stress,
With a baby, you will stress more and sleep less.

We went to Las Vegas and down the Strip,
It truly was an amazing trip,
We saw the casinos, classic cars
and more than one show,
I gambled a coin, yes I had a go,
On the way back, my scooter went slower and
slower,
Because its battery charge
was getting lower and lower,
Then it got worse and the batteries went flat,
So Steve had to push me the two miles back,
We went out from Las Vegas;
we hired a camper van,
This took us, all the way to the Grand Canyon,
We went to Chelly Canyon, Bryce Canyon
and many another,
I felt like Bryce Canyon was The Grand Canyon's
older brother,

We had to wear all our clothes one night,
Next day Monument Valley was pearly white,
This was because it was covered in snow,
The place was truly aglow,
I think if I had to choose,
Bryce Canyon was the best,
But I then change my mind,
when I think of the rest.

I went to Rio de Janeiro in Brazil,
And flew round Jesus, oh what a thrill,
At times, this journey felt out of reach,
But not when we went onto Copacabana Beach,

Suddenly a wave came that caught us with spray,
Steve noticed a man, very fast, walking away,
He ran after the man and got our cameras back,
Then took a free water and gave him a smack,
In getting them back, Steve worked on a hunch,
After it all, an onlooker said 'Good punch!',
As for me, I felt greatly relieved,
Because our cameras he had retrieved.

On our way to Machu Picchu,
We went to altitude in Peru,
There, we had to chew on coca leaves,
Because altitude sickness it relieves,
That night I said the noise, it must go,
So Steve crossed the room
and closed the window,
But in the night, we woke gasping for breath,
This was because there was no oxygen left,
Steve then opened the window
to let the oxygen in,
That was the priority, over any noise or din.

To get to Machu Picchu we got up pre-dawn,
It was totally black, no sign of the morn,
So in the end, I got only two hours' sleep,
This made me quite grumpy
and I wanted to weep,
It was 10 a.m. when we got there,
But it was totally inaccessible in a wheelchair,
A Peruvian man helped by carrying me round,
The whole of Machu Picchu did me astound,

This Peruvian man, he was called Frank,
And after he carried me, him I did thank,
We also gave him a really big tip,
Because I never once fell from his grip.

Next to Iguazú Falls in Argentina and Brazil,
I either hated it totally or thought it was brill,
Wow, the heat there was beyond belief,
So when the waterfall spray hit us it was a relief,
In that moment I went from hell to heaven,
I jumped from cloud zero to cloud eleven.

In 2005, my period was late,
I thought, oh I've mistook my date,
But then I started being sick,
And craving sausage, bacon, beans and chips,
Then the next day I drove
to McDonalds in the rain,
I was on a mega-healthy diet,
so this was a little insane,

But the baby had phoned womb service
and ordered some fat,
So there I was in McDonalds
eating fries and a Big Mac,
Realising I was pregnant,
I kept asking Steve to get me a test,
He did in the end, to stop me being a pest,

If pregnancy was a chess move
it would be checkmate,
I felt backed into a corner,
from which there was no escape,
Pregnancy made me want to run a mile,
So in order to cope, I went into denial,
Around this time there was
a great deal of synchronicity,
I told my grandad, he said,
baby's meant to be,
Synchronicity is something
beyond coincidence,
When the unlikely kind of make sense.

There was our baby on the very first scan,
I said, 'I can't have a baby',
Steve said, 'Yes you can',
Steve said, 'It's a boy and all will be well',
I wanted the pregnancy secret;
Steve just had to tell,
Little miss, I know my body, had got it wrong,
No not four weeks' pregnant,
I was eight weeks gone,
During my pregnancy I had 11 scans,
Steve came to eight; he was a good man,
The doctor said if I got to 32 weeks,
the baby was home and dry,
When I got there, I didn't know whether to laugh
or cry,
Laugh because, Wow! my baby would make it,
Or cry because, the thought of a baby, I just
couldn't take it.

On the day Marcus was born,
I went to a baby stall,
And I came away with nothing at all,
When I got to the car, tears did flow,
So Steve went back and bought, two babygrows,
Good job he did because at the end of that same day,
Marcus was born; our son was on his way.

At 36 weeks, my waters broke,
Was I having a baby or was this a joke?
We went to the hospital;
they put me on a machine,
I didn't feel pain, or cause a scene,
The monitor showed I was having contractions,
But in my body, I felt little reaction,

But then the discomfort got a bit worse,
So I pressed the buzzer and called a nurse,
The doctor came and said I was 6 cm dilated,
Was I happy, no I didn't feel elated,
The doctor said the feet are on the way,
For once in my life, I had nothing to say.

They whisked me off for a caesarean section,
The memory of which I feel little affection,
I went to surgery and was made numb
from the waist down,

Steve came in wearing a white mask
and green gown,
There was a lot of tugging and pulling in my
tummy,
It was bizarre; it felt weird and funny,
Then before I knew it
there was a baby on my chest,
And then immediately,
they put him on my breast,

Yes, that's right, it was a boy,
But at the time, I didn't really feel much joy,
He was four weeks early, a little premature,
For me, what a shock,
I'd never held a baby before,
That week was the longest day of my life,
Psychologically, I felt
I'd been stabbed by a knife,
I saw a psychologist because I felt very alone,
He said, I was just out of my comfort zone.

Around this time, Steve's Uncle Marcus
died and moved on,
So our Marcus was born
and another Marcus was gone,
Marcus was also Steve's second name,
So any other choice was rather lame,
I also had a Marcus in my family,
So the name fitted well into my family tree.

When we got home, we did shifts at night,
Sharing the task made Marcus a delight,
Marcus was an easy baby,
he came off the top shelf,
We couldn't plan Marcus, he planned himself,
Marcus's birth made quite a stir,
He appeared on *Look North* and *Calendar*,
He even made the *Daily Mail*,
I bought many copies when it was on sale,
The story became a magazine spread,
Throughout the land it was read.

When Marcus was a baby,
he met a girl called Tigga,
Now in Marcus's world she's a major figure,
She was in shop mobility, helping out her dad,
When she met Marcus, which made her so glad,
What she feels for Marcus is pure love,
She calls him her little bruv,
Like me, she tandem skydived out of a plane,
Maybe Marcus loves those who are insane,
But when she was about to jump,
she had a panic attack,
But jumped anyway,
she's thankful for that.

We wanted help with Marcus
when we went away,
To help look after Marcus night and day,
She immediately said, 'I want to do that',
Soon she was sunbathing, as she babysat,

Yes, before she knew it,
she was in the Florida Keys,
And she settled in there with great ease,
In Florida was sunshine, pelicans, key deer
and palm trees, Key West and Marathon
where we often ate Chinese

When swimming with dolphins she did scream,
For this fulfilled her lifelong dream,
Tigga is a remarkable lady,
I'm so lucky she fell in love with my baby,
She is beautiful, simply stunning,
She came out to the Keys five years running,
At the end of our trip, we went to Orlando,
This was where she was born to go,
I had to go on all the rides,
so they didn't have to queue,
I was really terrified but had to make do.

Believe it or not, I've touched the moon,
Now you think I'm crazy or a loon,
At the Kennedy Space Centre,
I touched moon rock,
That's a memory I think of a lot,
I swam with the manatees in Crystal River,
The water was cold, it made me shiver,
In the water they look like a WW2 bomb,
The swim was half an hour, not too long,
We had to take care with these docile sea cows,
When they are asleep,
waking them no one allows.

We went to Angel Falls,
where Steve proposed to me,
But he didn't do it down on one knee,
No, Steve recorded a video track,
Which he then wanted to show me back,
I said no, save the battery,
But eventually he showed it to me,
I was stunned, shocked,
gobsmacked and speechless,
Although I did somehow manage
to say yes, yes, yes.

We then went to the Equator in Ecuador,
It was place we couldn't ignore,
There, everyone weighs two pounds less,
It wasn't the diet, I must confess,
On one side of the line the
water went down anti-clockwise,
And on the other, the opposite, to my surprise.

We went onto Galapagos and saw penguins,
sea lions and seals,
The wildlife was amazing,
the photographs unreal.
We arrived at Easter Island on Christmas Eve,
Making Christmas at Easter I do believe,
Easter Island is in the Pacific,
Bouncing around the island, was pretty horrific,
But it was the only way to see
the figurehead Moai,
That was a sight I did enjoy.

When Marcus was two,
Steve and I tied the knot,
When I had pneumonia, I promptly forgot,
I said to Steve, we're not married,
with great indignance,
When I recovered,
I apologised for my ignorance,
When we got married,

I scootered down the aisle,
So, I truly did arrive in style,
I was in such a hurry, I left my Dad behind,
Thankfully, he didn't seem to mind.

At the time of our wedding,
we bought a nine-foot dinosaur,
In our garden we have a Velociraptor,
We got it as the bride needed something old,
For buying it, we're mad, or so we've been told.

I went to Mexico on honeymoon,
And went on the beach at Cancun,
We also went to Teotihuacan, Mexico,
Where there is an amazing echo,
So, when Steve did a loud clap,
The sound came rebounding back

Steve being Steve made his unique bird cry,
This made everyone, look up at the sky,
We went to Mexico City,
where there's lots to do,
And where we chose to visit the zoo,
We went to a site called Chichen Itza,
American tourists call it Cheesy Pizza.

We also went to Acapulco,
Where the divers in the sea do go,
Off the cliffs they dive,
I'm amazed that they survive,
They dive right in, going head first,
I could think of nothing worse,
I'm a skydiver but to me they're crazy,
To do that no one could persuade me.

My Norwegian best friend's called Ann-Cathrin,
I met her in Freiburg, she's as close as kin,
When we met, she said a friendly hello,
Then off to her room we did go,
Once there we had a Tasse Tee,
I met Ann-Cathrin on my first Freiburg day,
She's a brilliant friend, I was lucky to meet,
A better friend I could not seek.
Later we met up with her in Berlin,
When Marcus had just started, toddlin'.

In Berlin, we also met with Marie-Louise,
She understood Steve,
about which I was pleased,
Because she was like an auntie to me,
Someone I counted as close as family,
Even more importantly,
she met Marcus, our son,
We all got on well and had lots of fun.
To Hitler's death bunker, Steve loved goin',
But I preferred Marie-Louise
and her generous lovin'.

One time we went on holiday to Egypt,
And I really didn't like it one bit,
Because we went there in the height of summer,
As destinations go, it's not a front runner,
Everyone seemed to be after a tip,
And it seemed they'd do anything for it,
We got the feeling they'd sell their own mother,
Just to get a tip, and then order another,
The problem was, it was too damn hot,
And I must stay cool, no matter what.

We went around Cairo in a horse and cart,
We saw the pyramids, a work of great art,
In the museum we went to see Tutankhamun,
Or rather should I say, his sarcophagus tomb,
Then we went to the Valley of the Kings,
Steve got out of the taxi and quickly nipped in,
And for me to go there was no way,
Because it was an extremely hot day,

I couldn't break my golden rule,
That, at all times, I must stay cool,
So I stayed in the taxi with Mr Chips,
While Steve with the heat got to grips.

The heat was even worse in Luxor,
I really couldn't take any more,
All I needed was my hotel room,
Air-conditioning couldn't come
a moment too soon,
I was just desperate to cool down,
To make me more bearable to be around.

In the last few years before he died,
Dad had a stroke and more often cried,
He didn't know me or my brother,
The one person he knew was my mother,
He often said in the last years of his life,
To my mum, you are my wife,
It was a bit annoying because
he said it all the time,
But now it's a treasured memory, in her mind.

My grandma made it to 94,
My grandad, then 91, lived for 10 years more,
He learnt how to cook and run a home,
And adjusted to living on his own,
This took a good deal of inner strength,
When he talked about God,
he could go on at length,

My grandad heard poems spoken in the night,
Something that gave his life great insight,
He wrote the poems down
and published two books,
They're really worth reading,
worth taking a good look,
He ate mouldy damsons
and food past its sell-by date,
He didn't worry about it; he just got on and ate,
He lost his car keys
every six months without fail,
He saw God everywhere, even in junk mail.

Steve cooked and cleaned for our family,
He had to get up at night, to turn me,
Things have changed
now I sleep on a bean bag,
I have less leg spasm, for that I am glad,
Now I can generally sleep at night,
I usually sleep through all right,
Sleeping pills knock you out and give you a rest,
But if you can get real sleep, that's the best.

MS got worse and I had no energy
to drink or eat,
I was staring in the face of defeat,
Steve got palpitations caring for me,
And once ended up in A&E,
He thought he was having a heart attack,
But he wasn't, thank goodness for that.
I went below six stone;

I was as light as a feather,
They put the peg in my stomach,
now I just eat for pleasure,
Fortisip feeds saved my life,
But there's still a lot of trouble and strife,
I've made it back up to eight stone,
And with my brother caring for me,
I don't feel so alone,
Steve has built me a room downstairs,
This shows that he really cares.

I got pneumonia not once but twice,
It is an understatement to say,
it was not very nice,
I hallucinated that Marcus went to a club,
How mad my brain, good heavens above!
And at the club he had three cups of tea,
Yes, there was something very wrong with me,
Fortunately, I recovered and survived,
And I'm glad to still be alive.

Because I got pneumonia, funding was very fair,
Now they want to cut it, they don't care,
The NHS is being crippled by Jeremy Hunt,
The Secretary of Health, is an utter c**t,
My brother and Steve fought
to get funding for me,
It shows I have an amazing family.

My childhood cat, Jim, caught loads of mice,
My brother's job was careers advice,
He gave the job up to look after me,
Please test him for insanity,
My brother is my hero, he's my rock,
I'm very lucky such a brother to have got,
From the airport he picks up my folk,
One time, Marcus screamed
'Hello Uncle Coke!',
I'm surprised he wasn't arrested
and put in front of a jury,
But it's funny now and makes for a good story.

A couple of friends are Carol and Eddy,
I phone them every week, when I am ready,
Another friend is called Liz,
To her place, I often do whizz,
I go there in my WAV, Fiat Doblo,
Which I bought a few years ago.

As there's no action down below,
A lot of men would simply go,
But I'm happy to say my husband didn't leave,
That was not the way for my Steve,
I've since given Steve a hall pass,
So, he can have sex if he meets a nice lass.

He went to Thailand and met a girl called Wan,
In a bar in Bangkok, that's how it began,
After two and a half years, they did split,
Steve dumped her for talking to him like shit,

I called her my surrogate vagina
When being daft, it's my way of coping,
having giggled and laughed,
Also, I didn't want Steve to be a wanker,
But as for Wan,
I didn't want to thank her.
I don't bother with gin, but I like my tonic,
For a girl who doesn't drink
it's somewhat ironic

I'm with my carers from 9.40
to half past six,
I feel very lucky and thrilled to bits,
Then at 10, in Yvonne does creep,
And an hour later I go to sleep,
My carers are my brother,
Verney, Yvonne and Tash,
And sometimes at the café,
I have bangers and mash.

The local café is run by Pat,
And once a week at the café I'm sat,
Pat let me put my press cuttings on the wall,
Where they could be read, by one and all,
I also put up two parrots,
the café sign and some fake flowers,
This café is so popular
some people go there for hours.

One day I went to the café, I then said t'rah,
On the way home my leg hit a steel bar,
Paramedics came out
but I wish they hadn't spoken,
Because they maintained that my leg
wasn't broken,
All I know is, it hurt like hell,
And day by day my leg did swell,
A doctor came out and said
my ankle was sprained,
I trusted her because she was trained,

My leg was broken but nobody could tell,
I felt sick to my stomach and very unwell,
The only one to have diagnosed it right,
Was my brother, who saw the bones break.

Then Sophie, my peg nurse,
took one look at my leg,
You need an X-ray, that's what she said,
Six days and six nights of spasming pain,
Until the X-ray, a double fracture made plain,
I was lucky the bone
didn't punch through the skin,
That really could have done me in,

If only that steel bar my leg hadn't stuck,
I wouldn't feel, I'd been run over by a truck,
My broken leg was spasming for far too long,
But it has taught me that I'm incredibly strong.

Now it's painful in a purple pot,
But in bed I'm not going to rot,
So, whatever you do, don't wish me luck,
And I'll try my best to never give up,
Marcus and Tasha's son Trevonte are best bros,
They'll be friends for life, that much I just knows.

I've never understood why 'sick' is cool,
For me that was the thinking of a fool,
But Marcus said, 'I'm a cool sick mum',
Now being 'sick' bangs my drum,
Yes, Marcus says I'm a great mum, I
'd be happy with good,
Without him could I cope?
No, I don't think I would,
Marcus is blond, cute, happy and clever,
Do I regret having him, no, no way, not ever,
Looking back, Marcus didn't come,
a moment too soon,
And when Marcus arrived,
Steve was over the moon,
He said to Marcus, you can be anything you want
son, yes you can,

You can be gay, straight or bi-sexual just not a
Sheffield United fan,
So, in my house it's all Sheffield Wednesday,
It's 'up the Owls' all the way,
It's amazing, Marcus turned out really fine,
I still can never believe he's really mine,
Now he's already made the age of ten,
To all our jokes, my brother groans,
oh no not again.

My favourite food is shepherd's pie,
It's as good as the sky is high,
On Tuesday I smile when Carol
walks through the door,
She does my nails, she's my sister-in-law,
I enjoy seeing my mum; to me she gave birth,
And we both love to listen to
John Shuttleworth.

At my funeral I want nobody to have cried,
Because I've had a blast, one hell of a ride,
But because of Marcus, I don't want to leave,
And I'm still quite fond of Steve.

My Leap of Faith 2016
(Revised 2016)

I revised this poem in 2016 because the original no longer said exactly what I wanted to say about my leap of faith against MS.

The revised poem has only a few extra and tweaked lines but I needed to do this to reflect MY leap of faith. That my leap was about putting total faith in diet, nutrition and exercise to combat, and reverse, MS.

That MY leap of faith was in part about brainwashing myself that these things would work; they may well work on their own in the battle with MS, as having a healthy lifestyle that revolves around healthy eating and exercise must be good for you. The self-brainwashing part just re-enforced its success, a placebo effect maybe, but to me it can't totally have been that, though possibly much of it was, that's something that will never be totally quantifiable.

My Leap of Faith (revised 2016)

I feel like stones being ground to dust,
My weary bones so full of rust,
I feel my life out of control,
Battering my torn and tattered soul,
Forcing me just like a slave,
Onward to an early grave.

But in truth this will not be,
For MS is not the enemy,
Like an anchor in the dock,
My faith holds firm. I am a ROCK,
Holding me where I belong,
Alive, Surviving, Steadfast and Strong.

I reject old thoughts, fresh thoughts bring good
luck,
I want to live, and I will never give up,
I brainwashed my brain into positive thinking,
I faced my realities, I gave up drinking,
My mind often yearns for that easy 'quick-fix',
But I must resist, for it doesn't exist,
Diet, nutrition and exercise pays,
Self-belief and self-discipline are the only ways.
I believe in success despite the MS,

The victim is gone the more I strive on,
Through thick and through thin,
I WILL NEVER GIVE IN!
Despite all the strife,
I WILL LIVE MY LIFE!

I now have a formula I add to each day,
My journey to WELLNESS to keep MS at bay,
The pathway is stony. I stumble and fall,
And often I meet what feels like a brick wall,

But from this path I will not stray,
I BELIEVE there will always be a way,
To stop the progress of MS,
And transform the diagnosis to 'God Bless'.

So I ACCEPT all the tears and release all my fears,
And I cling to the rope that signifies HOPE,
I know I will bleed but I know I'LL SUCCEED,
I'll believe in fate's plan and I'll pray all I can.

I will shine like a STAR for I have come so far,
A twinkling LIGHT to help others with their plight,
MS may do its worst but my bubble won't burst,
WHACK AFTER WHACK, I KNOW I'LL BE
BACK!

I'll live my life, and laugh and learn,
For like a ROCK my faith is firm,
My goal is high to become fully well,
I reach for the sky! Only time will tell.

So, I'll live for today, ENJOY THE RIDE!
The rest is for God to decide,
I now BELIEVE MS will set me free,
And truly be the making of Me!

My Cat Jim
(2016)

Creating *My Life Poem* in late 2015 and early 2016 got me on a positive roll of filling my brain with positivity rather than moping in depression about the progressing MS. It also left a big hole when it was completed, what was I to do now it was finished?

After a few false starts, I realised that I needed to celebrate, in poems, those in my life who I had a deep emotional attachment to, but who were no longer with us.

Maybe there was a tiny selfish motive in this in that the memories would always be there if expressed in poetry, shared for myself in case I ever got to the horrendous MS position of not remembering them.

Maybe that was a tiny bit of it, but it was more about promoting those who have gone, sharing the positive impact they'd had on me; what that they shared with me. It was about sharing people who had helped me develop into the person I had become.

The first poem was naturally, therefore, not about a person! Entropy strikes again? Well, maybe a little, but only a little, as those of you who have pets know, they can often be more loving and human to you than humans are, hence why the first of these poems was about my cat Jim, the first love of my life.

My Cat Jim

Something happened when I was eight,
That for me was truly great,
We got a black and white cat called Jim,
Whose life in Somerset did begin.

My grandparents brought him up to The Fairway,
Where from then on, he did stay,
He was a cat like no other,
To me, he was more like a brother.

I found Jim to be very wise,
Great wisdom there, in his yellow eyes,
Then one day a tabby cat came to the door,
One we'd never seen before.

She meowed and meowed, Let me in please!
While on the news, there were Kurdish refugees,
So, we were kind and let her in,
And her life with us did begin.

We called her 'MeMe'
because her meow said that,
So, she became our second cat,
When Jim saw MeMe he looked bored,
And usually, her he just ignored.

Him, she really did not impress,
He tolerated her, never the less,
Seven years later, MeMe got run down,
We were sad she was no longer around.

For her, crossing that road
when she was run over,
Was like swimming the Channel
from Calais to Dover,
But Jim always made it look easy,
Whether it howled a gale or it was just breezy.

Jim had a lovely black and white coat,
He lived 18 years, old enough to vote,
My friend Julia had a cat we called MiJ,
Because he was Jim's mirror image.

He may have been Jim's reflection,
But between those cats there was little affection,
When they met, they would start mewling,
It sounded like they were duelling.

Actually, it was caterwauling,
But it didn't sound appalling,
They'd sing a beautiful duet,
Whenever they accidentally met.

At 18, Jim had kidney failure
and dodgy back feet,
So the vet came and put him to sleep,
His last meal was a cat food turkey dinner,
As it was yummy, it proved to be a winner.

He also got milk, cream, butter and cheese,
For which he begged: For me please!
Then the vet kindly ended his battle,
And his life expired with a death rattle.

My image of Jim is still very clear,
It's as if he were still here.

My Dad

I wrote this poem to remember my Dad so that my Mum, and everyone else, would know how proud I was of him, not just as my Dad but as the man he was throughout his life.

How I admired the inner man, the man whose honest core beliefs and morals didn't change, even after the stroke that restricted his ability to elucidate them.

In the poem, I hoped to describe him not just in a positive light but as a whole man, by including his idiosyncrasies and foibles. I wanted the picture portrayed in my words to be true and believable, of someone everyone could recognise as a human-itarian and not as a made-up story of a human.

I wanted to portray the true man, the true moral gent he was, who my Mum loved and his friends truly respected.

I hope I've succeeded and that the humble, giving, loving, caring man I admired comes through in this poem, so that people can know him, the real him, even if they didn't meet him in life.

My Dad
(2016)

My Dad was born in York,
There he learned to walk and talk,
Mum and Dad were really smart,
They went to Leeds University, 13 years apart,

At M.I.T. dad completed his Ph.D.,
So, the United States he did see,
At Sheffield University they did meet,
Maybe he thought she was rather sweet.

However, he was a little bit slow,
In letting his emotions show,
But eventually the two went out,
After many dates there was no doubt.

He knew Sally would be his future wife,
Who he'd love for the rest of his life,
On holiday they climbed up Cheviot Hill,
And on their way up, they ate their fill.

Those bilberries must have gone
to my Dad's head,
Because at the top, 'Marry me' he said,
They bought a house on The Fairway,
My Mum still thinks it was a wonderful day.

Dad lectured in mechanical
and process engineering,
But he was not at all God fearing,
He went to his church every Sunday,
Where with the congregation he did pray.

The God he knew was warm and kind,
The kind of God I'd love to find,
And going to church he never neglected,
By everyone he was well respected.

He was teetotal, he didn't drink,
His mind was always clear and able to think,
Nobody saw my Dad getting pissed,
My Dad was a true Methodist.

My Dad practised Christianity
in the way he did live,
He always seemed to have something to give,
With him you never seemed to be judged,
But from his morals he never budged.

Dad took older people to church in his car,
Because otherwise for them it was too far,
He took Mr and Mrs Hartley and Mrs Twaddle,
It meant the world to them,
for him it was a doddle.

He asked little old ladies
to help him across the road,
When they did so, the traffic slowed,
Dad seemed to know everyone in town,
Yes, they knew him, Dennis Brown.

Dad was heavily involved with Labour,
Vote for someone else – do me a favour!
In Hallam he stood as the candidate,
But the vote he got was never that great.

As a result, he never did win,
But he lost with a smile and a grin,
My mum lectured in Russian in the Arts Tower,
As kids we went there for the odd hour.

The lifts were unusual as they had no doors,
You had to jump off, they didn't stop at floors,
The first child born to them was a son,
Then two years later was born more fun.

This was a girl, which was me,
Who completed our family,
No, that's not true, that's not right,
Because something happened when I was eight.

We got a black and white cat that we called Jim,
Whose life in Somerset did begin,
My grandparents brought him
up to The Fairway,
Where from then on, he did stay.

My Grandparents

I wrote this poem to remember what my grand-parents meant to me and so that my Mum would know how much her parents meant to me. I knew only one set of grandparents, as my Dad's parents died before I was born. This made my maternal grandparents extra special, I think.

It was a way of telling Mum things about my life with them, which maybe she wasn't aware of, telling her how they loved me and why I loved them.

It was also a way to remember them as whole people, including their minor eccentricities, while also conveying to people who have never met them, the loving, real people they were.

My Dad was a real gent,
And was careful with the money he spent,
We weren't super rich,
but we never went without,
I had great parents, there is no doubt.

Dad never swore, he just said 'blurge baggers',
Even when telling us off,
his finger all a waggers,
Dad took me to athletics, orchestra and choir,
A lot of time this did require.

My Dad was usually very humble,
But at Wednesday matches he did grumble,
Sometimes Dad bought a quarter of sweets,
For me these were lovely treats.

For him sherbet lemons, for Mum pear drops,
For these were the sweets they liked lots,
My Mum loves a dark chocolate Bounty bar,
She thinks they are the best by far.

One time we went cycling as a family,
And many sites we did see,
We went to Scarborough,
Whitby and Boggle Hole,
Doing this trip was rather bold.
Especially after Dad toppled down a bank,
When I saw that my heart really sank,
Thankfully, he got up, there was nothing wrong,
So, we were able to keep cycling on.

On holidays and walks for energy's sake,
Mum would give us Kendal Mint Cake,
It helped us get up cliff and hill,
But following Mum was still quite a skill.

I asked for Mental Kink Cake when being daft,
In the middle of nowhere, we always laughed,
In sunshine, I would get a tan,
So of hot sun I was a fan.

But Dad 'Mr Brown' turned bright red,
So in the shade he stayed instead,
My Mum is vegetarian, so no meat was Dad fed,
If he missed meat, he never complained or said.

As he didn't make Mum prepare him meat,
Instead, it became an occasional treat,
My Mum's favourite numbers
are seven and three,
A love for these numbers she passed onto me.

My least favourite number was 42,
But Dad brilliantly changed it to fortitude,
Now that number doesn't bother me,
Anyway, I'll shortly be 43.

Dad was always on time, he was never late,
His favourite number was 88,
Dad loved the Ying Tong song by The Goons,
He'd sing it like a kid with party balloons.

Ying tong diddle I po, Ying tong diddle I po,
That is how the silly song did go,
He loved Geordies and Northumberland,
He loved Alnmouth Beach with its sand.

He really loved the Cheviots and the sea,
So up there my Mum, his ashes set free.

My Grandparents
(August 2016)

My grandparents lived in Northumberland,
I loved building castles in the sand,
We enjoyed going to the river Aln,
And seeing Percy the pelican,
We enjoyed going to that lovely river,
Seeing the pelican made us all aquiver.

What's the opposite of a pelican?
Try and guess, if you can,
I'll tell you, oh no I shan't!
Ok, I will, it's a pelican't,
Then my grandparents left Alnmouth,
They moved away, far down south.

They moved all the way to Somerset,
After this, holidays there, we did get,
They were happy on their arrival,
They moved to the village of Curry Rivel,
At Frankley Services, we'd meet them there,
Driving half-way each was pretty fair.

I enjoyed having sausage, beans and chips,
This was a rare treat and I loved it to bits,
Sometimes Grandma made us a promise,
That we'd go to Cricket St Thomas,
We saw lions, giraffes, elephants,
and monkeys too,
Many animals we did see at this wonderful zoo.

Sometimes we got up with the lark,
And went to Longleat Safari Park,
We had to go round by car,
But it was the best way by far,
To see wild animals roaming free,
And looking relaxed and very happy.

Sometimes the monkeys jumped on a car roof,
While other wild animals remained aloof,
Sometimes the monkeys
grabbed a windscreen wiper,
This was exciting and made us feel hyper,
Going round Longleat House
I found quite a bore,
Maybe because it was a very long tour.

We also went in Longleat maze,
But us it didn't ever faze,
Because my grandparents were so clever,
We didn't get stuck in there for ever and ever,
Yes, my grandparents were really quite smart,
And always got us home before it got dark.

My Dad was a real gent,
And was careful with the money he spent,
We weren't super rich,
but we never went without,
I had great parents, there is no doubt.

Dad never swore, he just said 'blurge baggers',
Even when telling us off,
his finger all a waggers,
Dad took me to athletics, orchestra and choir,
A lot of time this did require.

My Dad was usually very humble,
But at Wednesday matches he did grumble,
Sometimes Dad bought a quarter of sweets,
For me these were lovely treats.

For him sherbet lemons, for Mum pear drops,
For these were the sweets they liked lots,
My Mum loves a dark chocolate Bounty bar,
She thinks they are the best by far.

One time we went cycling as a family,
And many sites we did see,
We went to Scarborough,
Whitby and Boggle Hole,
Doing this trip was rather bold.
Especially after Dad toppled down a bank,
When I saw that my heart really sank,
Thankfully, he got up, there was nothing wrong,
So, we were able to keep cycling on.

On holidays and walks for energy's sake,
Mum would give us Kendal Mint Cake,
It helped us get up cliff and hill,
But following Mum was still quite a skill.

I asked for Mental Kink Cake when being daft,
In the middle of nowhere, we always laughed,
In sunshine, I would get a tan,
So of hot sun I was a fan.

But Dad 'Mr Brown' turned bright red,
So in the shade he stayed instead,
My Mum is vegetarian, so no meat was Dad fed,
If he missed meat, he never complained or said.

As he didn't make Mum prepare him meat,
Instead, it became an occasional treat,
My Mum's favourite numbers
are seven and three,
A love for these numbers she passed onto me.

My least favourite number was 42,
But Dad brilliantly changed it to fortitude,
Now that number doesn't bother me,
Anyway, I'll shortly be 43.

Dad was always on time, he was never late,
His favourite number was 88,
Dad loved the Ying Tong song by The Goons,
He'd sing it like a kid with party balloons.

Ying tong diddle I po, Ying tong diddle I po,
That is how the silly song did go,
He loved Geordies and Northumberland,
He loved Alnmouth Beach with its sand.

He really loved the Cheviots and the sea,
So up there my Mum, his ashes set free.

My Grandparents

I wrote this poem to remember what my grand-parents meant to me and so that my Mum would know how much her parents meant to me. I knew only one set of grandparents, as my Dad's parents died before I was born. This made my maternal grandparents extra special, I think.

It was a way of telling Mum things about my life with them, which maybe she wasn't aware of, telling her how they loved me and why I loved them.

It was also a way to remember them as whole people, including their minor eccentricities, while also conveying to people who have never met them, the loving, real people they were.

On other days we went to One Tree Hill,
Roly poling down was quite a thrill,
Sometimes we went to Burrow Mump,
Or it might be a different tump,
We also drove to Ham Hill,
Where we ran like a windmill.

All across Somerset we did forge,
Yes, we made it to Cheddar Gorge!
At Wookey Hole we went into the cave,
Doing this felt really brave,
On our helmets a light it shone,
So, we could see everything and everyone.

From the cave ceiling we saw stalactites,
And up from the ground there were stalagmites,
Sometimes these joined together,
Which was both beautiful and very clever,
Sometimes our parents joined us there,
And Somerset, with them we could share.
My Dad usually walked ahead very fast,
While my Grandad always trailed in last,
On his head always a deer stalker,
But it didn't make him a fast walker,
As notes he was always jotting,
Especially when he was bird spotting.

Or botanising plants and wild flowers,
He loved doing this; he could do it for hours.
Wherever he went, he took his binocs,
This was an item he never forgot.
Grandad led many an organised walk,
But only one to one did he talk.

This is because he was hard of hearing,
And many voices together were not endearing,
We'd walk along with our Grandma,
Until we reached their small car,
When we got in, Grandma gave us a treat,
A lovely mint toffee, a Murray Mint sweet.

Grandma made lovely picnics,
Which didn't include gin and tonics.
But cheese sandwiches, biscuits and lovely cake,
Which at home she did bake,
Sometimes around the dining table we did sit,
Where we enjoyed a game of pit.

We also enjoyed the game of speed,
Also, at my grandparents, a lot I did read,
I enjoyed the Secret Seven
and the Famous Five,
They solved many murders,
but did themselves, survive,
I also enjoyed reading Malory Towers,
I'd get engrossed and read for hours.

Sometimes we had a game of chess,
I seldom won, but enjoyed it never the less,
At Friends' Meeting everyone did assemble,
And my Grandad's leg there, often did tremble,
Yes, when he spoke his leg did a shaker,
So I suppose you could say
he was a true Quaker.

When at my grandparents,
we made coconut macaroons,
Holidays flew by and were over too soon.
Staying at my grandparents was the best,
And I believe my parents enjoyed the rest.

My Crazy Brain
(October 2016)

OK, let's be upfront about this poem – it isn't everybody's cup of tea! That's because it comes out of the silly, bizarre, entropic, brain-twiddling side of me.

How did it come to be written?

Well, because I'm me, but also because I've ended up being physically unable to do a lot for myself because of MS. This means I am bed ridden a lot of the time and even with good carers and watching soap operas, I can sometimes get bored. To alleviate the boredom, I have taken to entertaining myself in my own head with riddles, puns and jokes.

Riddles and weird thoughts make up this poem, it shows where my brain goes to entertain itself. If you like riddles and 'my' bizarre brand of humour, then it's for you, if you don't, then I apologise in advance for wasting a little portion of your life. Whether you like it or not I challenge you to give your own brain some of its own bizarre time. I'm sure you'll come out of it smiling and laughing, I always do when I think through this poem.

Embrace life, embrace its silliness, I dare you!

My Crazy Brain

If you were in a race,
And you passed the person in second place,
Would you be number 1?
If you think so, you'd be wrong,
No, you wouldn't come first,
You'd come second, but second is good, you could
be worse.

If there was a hole in the ground,
How much dirt in it can be found?
If you think any dirt at all,
That would be a very bad call,
Because of dirt there is not one speck,
Do you get the answer yet?
This is because in that hole,
It is empty, there is nothing at all!

What do you call a fly that is dead?
Not a fly, that cannot be said,
It is a flown,
Did that answer make you groan?!
What do you call a daddy long legs,
that has no legs?
It's no longer a daddy long legs now it's dead,
It's just a daddy all alone,
Just a daddy on its own.

What do you call a wasp that is dead?
It's not a wasp, that cannot be said,
It is a 'was' without the P,
So it could be the Queen B.

What do you call a bee that is dead?
It's not a bee, that cannot be said,
The bee that is dead has been,
It might even have been the Queen,
But not a legume,
You can consume,
It's more of a bin,
But not a bin you put your rubbish in,
More of a bin n gone,
Where you bin, Hong Kong?
Nowhere you (w)heely bin,
(w)heely bin Hong Kong,
Did it get there? No,
the bee didn't live that long,
As it's dead and not alive,
And no longer buzzes in a hive.

What do you call a flea that is dead?
It's not a flea, it's a fled.

What do you call a clown who's a twin?
The twin who is the double of him,
He's not a clown,
I told my friend Jaqui
on the phone,
He's less of a clown,
more of a clone.

What do you call a seagull that is dead?
It's not a seagull, that cannot be said,
It's a soargull, that's not true
because it doesn't soar,
In the air as before,
Maybe it's a seen,
Because it has been,
But whether dead
or alive in the rain
it gets soaked,
So I would call it
a seengulped.

Our Chemistry Teachers

Why does this poem exist? Probably because it brings back good memories of youth, and we all like those, don't we?

Memories of an embarrassing (or is it giggle-worthy?) teenage crush for a chemistry teacher that I shared with my best friend, a crush that coincided with our interest in and study of chemistry.

It's my memories of how we enjoyed studying chemistry, about what we learnt, and about who we learnt from.

It's quite self-indulgent as a poem I guess, but it's also true, honest and without guile, and maybe it raises the question: Did we study better and learn more because of our crush, or did we giggle too much and learn less?

Whatever the true answer to that question, we did both go onto study chemistry at university.

Our Chemistry Teachers
(October 2016)

Me and Sara fancied our chemistry teacher,
So in our lesson plans,
chemistry did feature,
We thought Mr Carroll
looked like Micky Rourke,
And we loved all the chemistry he taught,
He taught about S orbitals,
D orbitals, and P orbitals too,
And from this how, with bonds,
molecules grew.

His voice had an Irish lilt,
And he showed through bonds
how chemicals are built,
We used litmus paper and
with acid it turned red,
We were never allowed to work with the dangerous
element lead,
And with alkaline, it turned blue,
During lessons with him,
time simply flew.

In lessons when not using litmus paper,
We learnt how to turn liquid to vapour,
This was known as evaporation,
And going from gas to liquid,
was condensation,
We also did distillation,
which made chemicals more pure,
Chemistry we simply couldn't ignore.

When we put magnesium in flame
it burnt white,
It was spectacular, burning so bright,
Sodium burnt with an orange flame,
We knew each periodic element by name,
Hydrogen, helium, beryllium, boron too,
Carbon, nitrogen, oxygen and fluorine,
to name a few.

We often used the Bunsen burners,
We were bright and quick learners,
We also had a chemistry teacher
called Mr Conheeney,
On the blackboard, his writing wasn't teeny,
In fact, it was quite a scrawl,
When he drew his lessons
on the blackboard on the wall.

But despite this we managed to decipher,
And write our notes
without using a typewriter,
So we could understand,
All the lesson he had planned,
Once, Mr Conheeney came in,
And on his face was a really big grin.

Because he'd asked Miss Butler to marry him,
And she'd said yes, so her he did win,
They went on to have a son,
And then they had another one,
So they had two brothers,
First one and then another.

A Universe of Thought
(November 2016)

This poem was inspired by Stephen Hawking. Stephen Hawking the man, Stephen Hawking the scientist, Stephen Hawking –the Stephen Hawking.

To me, the above makes sense because the whole of Stephen Hawking's life inspires me.

Me, the scientist, thinks, 'Wow, how did he get his head round physics and come up with the theory of black holes?'

Me, the battler, thinks, 'Wow, how did he have the strength to battle motor neurone disease and live so many years longer than expected while still doing ground-breaking scientific work?'

Me, the battler, thinks, 'Wow, how did he do all that while not only being civil to people, but also going out, giving talks, being a humane human who naturally inspired people?'

What he did, was the starting point of the poem, but then you add me into it, my knowledge of science, my belief in science but also my philosophical side, the side of me that asks the questions about God, life, the universe.

Naturally, me being me, it's more than just philosophical questions that have gone into the poem, there are challenging thoughts and questions, hopefully done in a way that does not offend but makes you think, Why is that so? Should it be so?

In its way, it's also a celebration of all life, the wonder of it, the wonder of all thoughts, whether the thoughts are the wow thoughts of Stephen Hawking or the thoughts that you and I have, that make each other stop, listen and think 'Wow I'd never thought of that!'.

A Universe of Thought

Stephen Hawking has motor neurone disease,
But Einstein I think
he would have pleased,
As illnesses go, it's one of the worst,
He survived; a genius
thinking about the universe.

He's got a brilliant mind,
And wrote a book called
'A Brief History of Time',
Most people with motor neurone,
at most five years stay alive,
But amazingly for over 40 years
he has survived.

With his carer he had an affair,
At first his wife was unaware,
Then the love was plain to see,
And split up his family.

Time and space aren't real,
Psychic mediums tell us our spirits defy time and
about how they feel,
Ok that's probably mostly mumbo jumbo,
I think it probably is, but I don't know.

I'm not an atheist, I'm an agnostic,
My faith in God, I seem to have lost it,
I've had hands-on healing so many times,
It's never worked, no help, rather a bind.

The universe started with a big bang,
But did it just happen or was it planned?
It's best not to get stuck
in a black hole, no, never,
Because time slows down
and you'd get pulled apart for ever.

Since then, the universe continued to expand,
An infinite amount, did it just happen
or was it planned,
In our solar system, we live in the Milky Way,
How many galaxies in the universe,
nobody can say.

It's billions, far too many to count,
You add up for ever, so large the amount,
Too many to count, by far,
Millions, billions and even more stars.

When I went to university,
I got the nickname 'Entropy',
This is because I was chaotic,
And more than a little entropic.

So, the name 'Entropy', was given to me,
Entropy is a powerful force; it makes sugar dissolve
in tea,
Going from a state of order to disorder,
Like a garden full of weeds with no border.

Entropy makes the universe expand,
Did it just happen or God, did He plan?
If there is a God, I think God is love,
Maybe we'll find out in heaven above.

Or maybe, after we die,
Bad people go to hell and then they fry,
But I don't really believe in heaven or hell,
On that subject I don't like to dwell.

Because I have enough problems
getting through this life,
And causing friends and family
a lot of trouble and strife,
Stephen was a victor over his illness,
not a victim,
I think the Nobel Prize
should be given to him.

Stephen's work is theoretical,
on the edge of space and time,
And his problem is that it cannot be proven
or defined,
That's because we've got a finite brain,
So trying to understand infinity
really could drive you insane.

Maybe if Nobels were given by the Queen,
To Buckingham Palace he should have been,
But unfortunately, one cannot prove a black hole
exists,
Otherwise, his name would be first on that list.

Yes, his name would be first,
For all his work on the entire universe,
Did you know God's sexist?
Does He know ladies exist?
In church, you sing hymns not hers,

So, He favours not the madams but the sirs,
And at the end of a prayer,
it's not a-women but amen,
So, God favours men once again.

Did you know God had a name?
And it is not female, it is not Jane,
It's actually Peter because at the end of the prayer,
you say thanks Peter God!
My Dad in the chip shop
preferred haddock over cod.

It is amazing how the universe gave birth,
To all the planets, including Earth,
Earth's exactly the right distance from the Sun,
For life to evolve, to have begun.

Even though the Earth has a big tilt,
It's here, where all life was built,
Wow, on the Earth, life did evolve,
This story by Darwin to us has been told.

David Attenborough has studied
all kinds of species,
About which, I'm sure,
he's written many a thesis,

But not about me
and Marcus my son,
My reMarcusable boy,
my currant bun.
I now really celebrate
every New Year,
For surviving another,
I'm glad I'm still here!

Sylvie Wright
(An Extremely Stubborn Bitch)

This poem explores another part of my nature: stubbornness!

For better or worse, I can be stubborn, it's something I think that comes with me being a battler against MS, as stubbornness is the only way I know how to face it and
battle it.

I'm presenting me, warts and all, as I tend to blurt out what I'm thinking even when I really shouldn't. So, take the positive with the negative because it's me, and you can't split me like you can the atom.

I want people to know what it is I've had to face, where I have been, where I have had to come back from. If that is selfish then so be it, but I still need them to know.

I am not so self-unaware that I cannot see when stubbornness leads me down the blind alleys of stupid behaviour, so this is included in the poem too, as a warning. I guess I also wrote about this stupid stubbornness to admit to myself that I can do a lot of negative things, if I wrote them all down in a poem I couldn't deny them to myself, even if I'm not very good at counteracting them still.

I've also tried to weave into this portrayal of battling stubbornness, the positives in my life, of life, so people can see why I continue, why it's worth battling on, why it's good to be stubborn despite everything.

I want my life, my poems, and this poem to inspire others. Hopefully, this poem will inspire others to battle through whatever they are facing, disability or no.

Sylvie Wright
(An Extremely Stubborn Bitch)
(February 2017)

I got pneumonia not once but twice,
And I really don't want to make it thrice,
The first time I weighed less
than six stone in weight,
This left me in a very weak state.

I was living on the edge,
It was a very narrow ledge,
Because on top of pneumonia I got C-Dif
I was living on the edge
and then fell off the cliff.

They thought my problem
was that I could not swallow,
Life without food
left my world feeling hollow,
But the real problem was
that I couldn't be sick,
(That's right, I couldn't vomit.)

The Fortisip came up and then
went down the airway,
And then in my lungs it did stay,
Yes, that's how the infection did begin,
And how the Fortisip in my lungs got in.

At the time I felt like pneumonia had won,
I felt defeated because food got in my lungs,
Thankfully, I managed to recover,
I lived to fight another day and see many others.

At the time, I'd become very weak,
Because I was too sick to drink and eat,
But I couldn't give up on my life without a fight,
Even though I was very light.

Thankfully, I did not die,
It was not my time to say goodbye,
I didn't sleep for three whole nights,
And believe me after that, I felt very uptight.

I felt very highly strung,
And felt like pneumonia again had won,
The problem was I did hyperventilate,
My heart it beat at a very fast rate.

There was little chance of sleep,
And at the time I did weep,
I was so cream crackered,
That's right, I was totally knackered.

Recovery took three weeks,
Thankfully, I didn't admit defeat,
I had septicaemia and a UTI,
And in spite of all these I did not die.

I must be a cat with nine lives,
Because everything I seem to survive,
When I had pneumonia
many stories I reported,
And some of them
were very contorted.

I think I went a little bit insane,
How mad my random brain,
I saw my late grandma
whose maiden name was Bear,
I couldn't believe she was right there.

I couldn't believe my eyes,
It was a very big surprise,
She was sat in a wheelchair,
And the sight made me stare.

Did you know that mother-in-law
is an anagram of 'Woman Hitler'?
Now there was a very evil mister,
Yes, he was evil and twisted,
And the world a better place
if he'd never existed.

Now back on track with my sister-in-law,
When I got pneumonia at her I swore,
For that Steve said
he would pay me good money,
Because he found it really quite funny.

No, Carol is good,
Even with pneumonia, this I understood,
At the time I remember
a good-looking male nurse,
And with him I sometimes did converse.

Since this time, I've lived many years,
But my life is still often
controlled by fears,
Now, I am quite healthy,
and I'm a good weight,
So I'm no longer
in a very bad state.

I have my carers from 9 til' 6,
I love them all to bits,
I have a carer called Maverney,
And when I misbehave,
she speaks to me sternly.

I only misbehave when I'm tired,
And my nerves feel hot-wired,
I eat now four times a day,
Every time I do, to Maverney, thanks I say.

Because she's a brilliant cook,
On her food I am hooked,
Maverney – I call her Vern,
And when I misbehave, boy do I learn.

But she gives me outstanding care,
Of that I'm very aware,
Steve calls her Vinny,
And when cleaning she wears a pinny.

I've got a carer called Tasha,
As carers go, she's a fire cracker,
Tasha can be very 'blonde',
Of her son, Trevonte, I am very fond.

I forgot to mention Yvonne,
To my care team she also does belong,
She does the odd Saturday
but mostly puts me to bed at night,
Then back to her house, she takes flight.

The problem now is that I have become addicted to
the burp,
And for my carers I can be
very hard work,
Yes, I always want to burp,
And it drives everyone berserk.

How many times do I burp a day, sometimes it's
best not to ask this question,
And the b word it is often best not to mention,

I'm sure at times Vern and Tasha
want to throw me in a ditch,
But I'm still here because
I'm an extremely stubborn bitch.

I am a burping addict,
I've got a terrible burping habit,
I even swallow air to make myself burp,
I must be a complete and utter twerp.

Regarding burping, I now feel conflicted,
Because burping 18 hours a day is unrealistic,
I mean it's ok to burp once in a while,
But I burp like it's going out of style.

I burp like it's the latest fashion,
To control this, watermelon,
my carers do ration,
I love to eat all the watermelons
the shops are selling,
How much a day,
now that will be telling.

Burping makes no logical sense,
When burping I feel like I'm in a prison surrounded
by a gated fence,
I'm in prison surrounded
by a fence and locked gate,
From this prison I really want to escape.

Yes, I really want to break free,
To improve mine and everyone's life quality,
So, steps I am taking,
Towards this habit to be breaking.

Vern says you'll never change,
you'll never learn,
But all I can say is watch me, Vern,
We'll see what happens;
I want my life to be ace,
So all I say is, people watch this space.

I know I don't have to burp,
but I don't yet believe it,
But at least now I can conceive it,
As apparently, it's a learnt behaviour.
Vern's food is full of flavour,

Vern's food is always made fresh,
I love it, it is the best,
I was trying to work out how sick could ever be
good, or ever be cool,
But then I thought, I'm good and I'm sick so all I
say now is 'Sick Mums rule'.

Thankfully, nowadays each day
I only have one Fortisip,
I have to be careful that it doesn't make me sick,
Because if it does,
I have this problem with phlegm,
And I always think, oh no not again.

In life I try to look at the glass half full,
not half empty,
But even half full, I think that is still plenty,
I overcame my half-womb
when I had Marcus, my son,
And in that instant, I became a mum.

I couldn't go out and get a job
because of the MS,
So I put Steve on the net
and made him a big success,
So I'm very proud of myself,
Because I did that in spite of poor health.

And in doing so, I made Steve and I quite rich,
And I'm still here,
as I'm an extremely stubborn bitch,
Do you know why Steve is mad?
Because he's had to be both Mum and Dad.

All my friends are completely quackers,
And all my friends are as mad as hatters,
A bit like a paddling duck,
I survive, I never give up.

In recent years, MS has progressed a lot,
And far worse, I have got,
Now to transfer I use a hoist,
And every day I'm alive, I rejoice!

Yes, sometimes I can be rude,
selfish and neurotic,
It's a shame for anxiety
there is no antibiotic,
I still seem to press the button self-destruct,
And that really does screw me up.

Tasha's Trevonte said, given the life I've led,
I should be more confident,
yes that's what he said,
He says I should believe in myself more,
And then 3-1 against MS is the final score.

I feel like I've already won,
Because so many places I have been,
and the things I have done,
Yes, I feel like a winner,
With MS at 21, I was just a beginner.

But now that I'm 43,
I'm an MS OAP.
To be alive, I feel fortunate,
I go on because I never give up.

I know after 22 years,
MS cannot be fixed,
But I go on because
I'm an extremely stubborn bitch.

An Ode to John Shuttleworth

This poem was, obviously, inspired by the character John Shuttleworth because it's an ode to him and about him.

But why John? Why not someone else?

Well, laughter is one obvious answer, because what John does and who John is, makes me laugh. His mixture of truth and honesty works so well with his ineptness, which is actually just pure, golden quality.

I love the way he tries so hard but is hindered by those around him, not just by his family but also by his agent, Ken, who should really be a help. But John does not see it at all, he has a blind spot to it. He's nice to them all and works around them and therefore does not 'professionally' edit them out as he really should.

You can't even criticise those around him too much, as they are part of what makes John Shuttleworth work, he'd be nothing without his friends and family. He really is a guy you can imagine living down your street, in my case literally, as John, like me, is from Sheffield, South Yorkshire.

I think that to really appreciate this poem, you have to know something about John Shuttleworth and his songs and sketches, as the poem alludes to things that happen in them. I do, however, have a secret hope that it may inspire you to watch his CDs and DVDs, and lead you to something special, as special as he is for me.

An Ode to John Shuttleworth
(April 2017)

This is a poem about John Shuttleworth,
Who for me is a great source of mirth,
All the voices for John
and his family are done
by Graham Fellows,
John's wife, Mary,
you could never describe as mellow.

Graham does all the voices
for John's family and friends,
John often drives Mary around the bend,
John would deny that Graham Fellows exists,
After all, he's not on the shopping list.

At times, John's wife can be quite scary,
And of her, John's quite wary,
John is a versatile singer-songwriter,
But I think he's more of a lover than a fighter.

At the start of their relationship,
John won Mary's heart,
You could see that there was quite a spark,
As their relationship started, there was romance,
Especially when John took her out to a dance.

But now they are passed
the honeymoon stage,
Now they've reached middle age,
In their relationship, Mary wears the trousers,
Nowadays, John is quite good
at using web browsers.

Their son's name is Darren,
And their daughter's name is Karen,
Both their kids are almost grown,
And Darren, the nest has already flown.

He moved in with Plonker, as his house mate,
So, if he chose, he could go to bed late,
Darren works at Victoria Wine,
John drops in for plonk, from time to time.

Once, John wanted Mary and Karen
to dance the Irish jig,
But they wouldn't, which made John feel
not very big,

But then out of the blue,
They started dancing; their legs simply flew.
As they did the Riverdance,
Around the room they did prance,
By Mary, great food is John fed,
And when it's late she says
"John, time for bed".

He always says "I'll be there in a mo,
I've nearly finished recording my latest show".
To his shows he is a slave,
But with Mary he rarely misbehaves.

But once Mary shouted,
"Its 3 a.m. John, it's very late.",
Personally, I think John Shuttleworth
is so rubbish he's great,
She shouted when they were purchasing a toaster
on eBay,
The worry about winning, up made him stay.

They had put down a maximum bid,
For a penny short of a quid,
But unfortunately, this item they did not win,
So a new toaster search had to begin.

Thankfully, another one was found,
This one for a penny short of a pound,
And even better, it had a higher spec,
Pleasing Mary, by whom John is very hen pecked.

Even better, they could travel
to pick it up by car,
Because Hathersage was not too far,
So they drove via Burbage,
out in the countryside,
They had a really lovely ride.

This also saved on the postal cost,
So John was glad the first toaster bid was lost,
Even though up late he did stay,
Worrying about that bid on eBay.

Every few months, he empties the crumb tray,
This instruction from Mary he does obey,
Sometimes John gets a gig from his agent, Ken,
And John says, "Oh great, Ken, when?"

But his audience usually doesn't fill an arena,
One time he failed to get Mary
a new vacuum cleaner,
She was so upset, John she left,
And when she was gone John felt bereft.

Without Mary, John was completely lost,
So he always gets new vacuums,
whatever the cost,
Generally, John gets gigs at a nursing home,
And he's often stood there on his own.

John is accompanied by a keyboard,
And is rarely asked to do an encore,
John doesn't get paid;
he just gets petrol money,
I don't think that Mary finds that funny.

They may often have only
two pennies to rub together,
But I don't think they'll split up,
no not ever,
Mary works as a dinner lady
in a primary school,
And generally, John's wife thinks he's a fool.

So for John, money is often quite tight,
With his wallet feeling rather light,
I don't think you could describe John as cool,
But for me he's definitely a loveable fool.

Sometimes, John's constant music gets
Mary's head ringing,
She just wants him to stop
his music and singing,
She's says "Oh John, shut up, love,
You're doing my head in,
good heavens above".

She must have the patience of a saint,
But a saint we know she really ain't,
So sometimes, John buys Mary flowers,
Especially when he's gone on for hours.

He's very well behaved
and always does his chores,
And Mary he simply adores,
With her, he's really rather under the thumb,
To me, he's a great source of fun.

I don't care that some people
might call him cheesy,
Because his antics really do, please me,
He's definitely my cup of tea,
He makes me laugh; he is funny.

Ken his agent has a rather squeaky voice,
But for me, he's my favourite
character of choice,
You never see Ken, just the back of his hair,
Waving his arms around in the air.

He had a wife, but they always did argue,
Probably even over a nice barbecue,
Later, Ken was filled with remorse,
But it was much too late, so they are divorced.

Ken likes his takeaway curry,
To eat it, he always comes home in a hurry,
He also likes his Peshwari naan bread,
Once his friend Roger smashed a popadom on his
head.

Ken went on a talent show,
And had a jolly good go,
Unfortunately, he didn't come first,
In fact, he was the worst!

That's right, he came dead last,
But while playing his saxophone, he had a blast,
The show was called New Faces
and was in 1973,
After coming last, Ken was not at all happy.

They have a neighbour friend called Joan Chitty,
Where do they all live? Only in Sheffield City,
Once Joan helped paint the windowsill,
But at this job she was not very skilled.

So, she got paint on the window pane,
And when Mary got back, John got the blame,
Loitering youths,
Surly and aloof.

Not the types of lads you want to meet,
After dark in the street,
Their time is not well spent,
They're loitering with intent.

They hang around the off-licence
and somehow get booze,
These loitering youths,
One time, John wanted to buy, for Ken,
a birthday bench,
But he had two lovely wicker chairs,
so no, was his defence.

But John said on the chairs was mildew,
Ken said, "No, that's crayon,
done by my nephew.",
I always wonder what was true,
Nobody for sure really knew.

We know what John really thought,
The crayon story he never bought,
Yes, this one story he did not buy,
He just thought, oh Ken, nice try.

Later, John said, "I'm putting your present through
the door.",
A bench, through the door, made Ken unsure,
The present came through the letterbox,
What it was had Ken foxed.

It wasn't a birthday bench hitting the floor,
It was just a pack of drinking straws,
They cost just 15 pence,
So Ken said, "Where is my birthday bench?".

Then Ken said something rather bold,
"Well, the bench I could have sold",
John said, "You can't sell a gift.",
About this idea, John was seriously miffed.

John wanted to enter
the Eurovision Song Contest,
Because he felt his song
'Pigeons in Flight' was the best,

Of the song contest, John is a big fan,
He'd enter for Norway
who always got 'Nul Point'.

But he couldn't, they said there was no way,
That he could enter and sing for Norway,
So instead, he got a Norwegian
Who is called Jahn Teigen.

He'd sung for Norway
in the competition before,
Though as a Norwegian,
he got a very low score,
But, Jahn, he murdered John's song,
For John thought he sang it all wrong.

He did this by singing it far too high,
So, John to Jahn had to say goodbye,
He had to bid Jahn adieu,
And start to look for somebody new.

He found Katrina and the Waves,
And she his Eurovision dream did save,
But I suspect it was all just a dream,
When Katrina became his Eurovision Queen.

When everyone gave her douze point,
And all of Europe,
of John's song became a fan,
With John, I'm a number 1 fan,
Of this very funny man.

Mainly Marcus

This poem, mainly about my son Marcus, is the nearest I will ever come to writing a celebratory poem. I say this because it's about the one thing that means most to me in my life, my best achievement: giving life to my son.

It is a celebration of him, of my giving birth to him and my relationship with him; more than that, it's a celebration of his and my relationships with the rest of the family.

Maybe, therefore, it's also a bit self-indulgent. Ok, it definitely is, and I make no apologies for that. I hope and believe it's honest too, as it doesn't sugar-coat anything, just celebrates our family's life together.

Enjoy the celebration.

Mainly Marcus
(June 2017)

Before I had Marcus,
I'd have preferred a girl,
Now I wouldn't change Marcus for the world,
When Marcus was born, I'd have been happy to
give birth to a kitten,
But pretty soon after, by my son Marcus
I was smitten.

Before Marcus was born,
before I was a mummy,
When he was inside me,
in my tummy,
You could feel him rejoice,
Whenever he heard his daddy's voice.

As up went his little heartbeat,
It was as if his Dad he couldn't wait to meet,
They have a very strong bond,
And of each other are very fond.

They both feel for each other,
infinite love,
And it is a beautiful thing,
like two turtle doves,

With Marcus, I love the way Steve says
"Right, sonny boy",
And for me and Steve,
Marcus brings a lot of joy.

When I told my Dad, I was pregnant
he said "Oh dear",
It seemed to me he didn't want to be near,
He walked away into the back of the house,
Things went very quiet; as quiet as a mouse.

But then he came back
and me did congratulate,
For being in a pregnant state,
He gave me a kiss on my cheek,
Which I think was pretty sweet.

To school Marcus has never been late,
Which is truly great,
And his attendance at school is 100%,
And my Dad when alive was a true gent.

He was the exact opposite of Steve,
But I think with Steve,
he was quite pleased,
When I rang my parents
to tell them I was engaged,
It was when Steve was 51,
just past middle age.

And my Dad said "How wonderful",
He was very pleased, I could tell,
Yes, he was definitely pleased,
That I was engaged to my Steve.

Although he never complained
about us not being married,
I think over the threshold
he wanted me carried,
He never complained or said,
But he was very happy
on the day we were wed.

And my Mum, she said,
"…and what did you say?"
She didn't assume that I'd said "Yay",
I told her I said yes,
I think she might have guessed.

When I had Marcus it was a shock,
Thankfully, the trauma
of the caesarean I forgot,
Into sleeplessness and motherhood
I was thrust,
And it took me a little while to adjust.

At six weeks old he started to smile,
He smiled like it was the latest style,
When at three months old
he started to roll over,
I was happy, like a kid
who'd found a four-leaf clover.

When Marcus was a baby, he once screamed
for three hours on his own
Then he realised there was no point,
as he was alone,
He never did that again,
When he found nobody came.

Steve is a strong father figure,
And Marcus in his walker at him did snigger,
Marcus didn't usually laugh in bed,
But always squealed when landing
upon Steve's head.

His squeals of joy, louder than any cat,
The best memory of my life was that,
We've been lucky with Marcus, with nature,
And Steve has been great with nurture.

He is quite strict,
And to Marcus he can be a bitch,
Obviously, I'm having a joke,
Steve is a good dad
and a good bloke.

But sometimes with Marcus
he had to be strict,
Because bad behaviour
had to be fixed,
Eliminate it, don't tolerate bad behaviour,
Did Steve put up with it? Do me a favour!

Steve, bad behaviour had to eliminate,
Especially as my health wasn't that great,
Fortunately for us,
Marcus has always been very mature,
Much more than Steve and me,
that's for sure.

At nursery, he went to the adults,
to him that was common sense,
Marcus has never been short of confidence,
Marcus has always been blond,
cute, happy and clever,
Do I regret having him?
No, no way, not ever.

He's a really cute kid,
The best thing I ever did,
Marcus was an accident,
not a mistake,
And if he was,
the best one I've ever made.

At six months, he started to crawl,
Even though he was still very small,
He crawled up every stair,
And of the danger, Steve was aware.

So he walked up behind him,
As his mobile life did begin,
At 10 months old he started
to sleep through the night,
For Steve this was a real delight.

No more sleepless nights, from 10 months old,
For Steve, he's always been as good as gold,
With him in his walker,
along by my scooter I did him drag
It was a funny sight;
he was a good lad.

We went, me and Marcus,
I pulled him along,
That's why, together we did belong,
Often, we went to Tesco,
By scooter and walker,
off we did go.

I chanted "I'm buying bread
for Marcus Wright",
To help him sleep all through the night
And when in Tesco,
Marcus was not very quiet,
I'm surprised he didn't cause a riot.

Because he liked picking up food
from the shelves,
In the shelves, he often did delve,
Another time with Marcus I went to town,
There I scooted all around.

Then with the scooter, I didn't see the kerb,
Until it was too late for me to swerve,
I was going to Argos to get Shaun the Sheep,
When you pulled the lamb's tail, it gave out a bleat.

But we didn't get Shaun the Sheep that day,
After the accident, there was no way,
In the accident, I fell,
So Marcus fell as well.

Thankfully, Marcus he did bounce,
And a passing lady on him did pounce,
Next minute he was eating Jelly Babies,
I will always be grateful to this lady.

So I got in the ambulance and went to A&E,
Yes, we went to accident and emergency,
There they found, I'd broken my thumb,
Believe me, that day was no fun.

The next day I went back and they did operate,
For they had to set my thumb bone straight,
This meant I got a lower arm pot,
I wish by the kerb I had stopped.

I made it to Florida and it was still good fun,
I couldn't swim but I could still enjoy the sun,
In six weeks, the pot came off
and again I could swim,
My life with swimming could again begin.

At thirteen months old,
Marcus let go of the wall,
And I was afraid that he would fall,
But no, he took his first-ever steps,
I was amazed;
it's a moment I'll never forget.

Pretty soon everywhere he did walk,
And me and Steve he did stalk,
Everywhere he went a-toddling,
Following us like a duckling waddling.

When Marcus was a toddler
he couldn't say 'again',
So every time he said 'undeng, undeng',
At the age of four,
Was the first time Marcus swore.

He said, "It's fucking raining",
and he said it correct,
He was careful in the swear word he did select,
Steve asked, "Marcus where did you hear that
word?"
From you Dad, is where he said he'd heard.

So, Steve could hardly be mad,
As he'd learnt it from his 'great' dad,
In fact, I think Steve felt quite proud,
Though swearing, Marcus usually says,
is not allowed.
On swearing, he is quite tough,
He thinks, "Enough is enough",
He says to me, "Language, Timothy",
He prefers English to be swear free.

Marcus my son is 11 years old,
And generally, he's as good as gold,
But in the mornings sometimes his teeth he forgets
to brush,
And getting off for school is in a rush.

At school, Marcus is good at maths,
And is near the top of his class,
He usually gets a very good report,
And at Dobcroft, by great teachers, he is taught.

I pick him up from school,
Usually on Tuesday as a rule,
Once on the way home, Marcus said
"Mum give me a sum",
So I quickly thought of one.

What is, I asked, "144 squared?"
Most kids, to answer,
would not have tried or dared,
By the time he got home, he'd worked it out,
He checked with a calculator
so there was no doubt.

He'd got it exactly right,
Much to my surprised delight,
Also, animal, vegetable or mineral
is a game we play,
Who is best I will not say.

Actually, my brother at this is the best,
And minerals I can never seem to guess,
Yes, my brother usually comes first,
Marcus comes second
and I am the worst.

We also play the word association game,
get back to the word, the very same,
Then the game you have won, pick a new word,
and a new game is begun.

Grandma and Marcus are very close,
And he's the grandchild she loves the most,
I know she only has one, so he's also the worst,
But grandma would only say he comes first.

The worst, no Grandma would never say that,
She adores Marcus and thinks he's a grand chap,
Marcus has got mine and Grandma's brain,
And no, that doesn't make him insane.

He likes making up many a pun,
I think he's beautiful, not just handsome,
At school he needs help
with handwriting and grammar,
These he works on with his Grandma.

As a toddler, he used to call Grandma, 'gangma',
She thinks, the best name ever given her
by far, far, far,
Marcus loves what he was named,
And the name he would never change.

He would give himself the name Marcus,
And he's no longer afraid of the darkness,
He's getting tall now and soon
over Grandma he will tower,
He's like a beautiful blossoming flower.

Marcus can twist his Grandma
round his little finger,
And she thinks, at Christmas,
he's a great carol singer,
Marcus and Grandma go on long walks,
And when they do, they have good talks.

When Marcus and my mum
go down to the stream,
It's a very picturesque scene,
Sometimes they walk to the rock,
Actually, they do that quite a lot.

Marcus loves not so much dogs but cats,
He's happy when Grandma's Cleo
is sat on his lap,
She's a cat that doesn't meow,
No, she definitely says "Cleow".

Marcus is right, Upperthorpe's name
needs to be changed,
Because it's not very well named,
As it's at the bottom of a steep hill,
So the naming of this area is not so brill.

He's right, the name that should be taught,
Is that it's called Downerthorpe,
Marcus has started playing the trombone,
And no, the sound doesn't make me groan.

He's good because he's got very long arms,
And when he plays, I don't feel alarmed,
He's also about it very enthusiastic,
It's like he's playing trombone gymnastics.

What I love about Marcus most
is his zest for life,
He makes my life worth
all its trouble and strife.

Mum and Me Entwined

The original idea for this poem was to show my Mum how much I love her and how much she means to me.

The entwined bit is because the poem didn't work when I just wrote about Mum, for at the time of writing my emotions linked me and mum so tightly that I couldn't separate us, so the poem had to include both of us.

I think a major reason for this is that we've both had serious illnesses over the years, her cancer, from which she thankfully recovered and me MS, which is still here, worst luck. We're entwined because we've both been through a lot, which brought our emotions much closer together, forged them and entwined them.

The poem is written from my emotional point of view, so there is more about me in it than there is about Mum because, despite the previous poems I have written, there was still more I needed to say about how MS affected me and how difficult a battle it can be emotionally.

The poem starts with my Mum because her getting cancer and my reaction to it, preceded and overlapped with the beginning of the onset of MS for me. The poem ends with my Mum as she is so important that she must be the last thing I talk about, not me.

I hope my love for my Mum shines through and that you can see her personality in the poem, and that my life doesn't over intrude and dominate at her expense.

Mum and Me Entwined
(August 2017)

In 1993, Mum felt a lump in her breast,
And knowing this, I was stressed,
At first the doctors couldn't give an answer,
But then they told us it was breast cancer.

My mum had radiotherapy and chemo,
I just wanted the cancer to go,
Thankfully, the cancer
to her lymph nodes hadn't spread,
The word 'cancer' filled me with dread.

I was really scared she would die,
I really felt I needed to cry,
Emotional stress, Mum,
Cancer. Why? Why? Why?
Then they got the chemo dose far too high.

I was definitely not at my best,
But to Mum, didn't want to be a pest,
They killed off all her white blood cells,
My mum was very sick and unwell.
Mum had a blood transfusion,
My life, MS, full of stress and confusion,
All these new symptoms of MS,
I was definitely not emotionally at rest.

During treatment, my Mum wore a wig,
Once, it got hooked up on a twig,
When she noticed, she could hardly believe it,
Even as she went back to retrieve it.

The wig was not the best style
But when I tell this story, i
t makes people smile,
Thankfully, the chemo worked,
she was eventually cured,
I started with MS, oh how I hated those words.

Thankfully, the cancer was fixed,
My mum is now 76,
Talking of MS, my vision did shimmer,
At 21 I was an MS beginner.

Yes, it was a little blurred,
And my speech at times was a bit slurred,
With MS, to look at me you couldn't tell,
That I was at all unwell.

But I knew what was wrong,
And to the MS community
I didn't want to belong,
I felt off balance and dizzy,
To cope, I kept myself busy.

I knew MS was bad news,
And I was feeling battered and bruised,
Often, with fatigue in my bed I collapsed,
Dreading the thought of an MS relapse.

I felt like my life had been shattered,
I knew exactly what was the matter,
I was very young and scared,
For life with MS I wasn't prepared.

MS for me was a living nightmare,
It all seemed very unfair,
At university I still enjoyed an odd beer,
But MS was still my greatest fear.

Sometimes I didn't want to get out of bed,
It didn't help
that a psychologist in Germany said,
"Die Augen mussen sehen wollen",
And in Germany I sometimes ate stollen.

I think she meant my problem was anxiety,
This meant I did not see clearly,
It made me hyperventilate,
Breathing at too fast a rate.

It made my vision shimmer,
I didn't at this time feel like a winner,
But with her I did disagree,
There was another reason I could not see.

Because the signal from my brain
was interrupted,
Meaning my vision was disrupted,
In Freiburg I went into a clinic for tests,
After a week of this I was unwell and stressed.

Into the clinic I did go,
When they said possible MS, I thought 'Bingo!'
My legs and arms did tingle,
I wasn't happy because
I was alone and single.

I knew MS was bad news,
Sometimes to cope, I drank booze,
To numb myself from the pain,
And to stop driving myself insane.

After a hangover, I felt shattered,
Totally knackered, cream crackered,
I also had awful fatigue,
In the final year, it mademy notes and books
more difficult to read.

I was on this awful rollercoaster ride,
I went numb on the torso on the left-hand side,
On this awful living rollercoaster,
I felt like a piece of bread being burnt inside a
toaster.

I was very scared – nightmare,
The cross of MS, I found very hard to bear,
Life seemed so unfair,
Facing MS, I didn't dare.

I thought that I had very bad luck,
And if I'm honest, I wanted to give up,
I just wanted to run away,
But, of course, with MS you've got to stay.

You can't run away
You must face the day,
In my final year,
I put my head down and studied,
With symptoms of MS, I was very worried.

In my final year, from MS I wanted to flee,
What really helped me, were classes of tai chi,
It helped the chi flow round my body,
I could then run home; I was symptom free.

It was as if there was nothing wrong with me,
It also reduced my anxiety,
It made me grin within, with glee.
Yes, I was that happy.

I studied hard and I came second in the year,
In spite of undiagnosed MS,
which was my big fear,
I got a First,
Very far from the worst.

When I graduated from Sussex University,
I graduated in German and chemistry,
When I got diagnosed with MS,
I really was not feeling my best.

I'm the first case of MS in my family,
No, no one with MS in my family tree,
After my MS diagnosis, I climbed Win Hill,
Keeping up with Mum was quite a skill.

But I got right to the top,
That's a memory I think of a lot,
To a rock called the headstone,
I went out-of-doors,
I had to walk across the moors.

I battled through the wind and rain,
Those who saw me
must have thought me insane,
When I got to it, I climbed to the top,
Of this quite tall rock.

Between Mum's chemo's,
my Dad and Mum went to China,
I don't think mum and dad
had a trip that was finer,
They also went to the States,
And they thought that trip was great.

At 23, I got my MS diagnosis,
And progressive MS was not a good prognosis,
I felt of my future, I'd been robbed,
And regularly about this I sobbed.

I felt all battered and bruised,
As well as feeling very confused,
I felt all bruised and battered,
And that my future had been shattered.

MS continued its progression,
It led me to severe depression,
Mum is no longer sick,
She doesn't need a walking stick.

She goes out walking on the moors,
She loves being in the great outdoors,
She loves walking by the heather,
She walks, no matter what the weather.

My Mum from walking so much is very fit,
That's truly understating it,
You know when I did my skydive,
I felt truly alive.

Doing it was quite a ride,
Something I'm glad I did survive,
At the time everyone said I was brave,
But my life the skydive did save.

I did it at the time, as I wanted to die,
That's why I flew out of the sky,
When skydiving, everyone
has two parachutes,
And when I skydived, I wore a jumpsuit.

From 13,000 feet,
From that high I did leap,
I must admit it was pretty sweet,
As well as being pretty neat.

Freefall was for a couple of minutes,
not that long,
Fortunately skydives, they rarely go wrong,
There is truly little danger,
Less than a car ride with a stranger.

Or just getting into a car,
And travelling any distance, short or far,
Or even crossing the road,
Even when the traffic has slowed.

So overall, it wasn't so brave,
But it did lead to my life being saved,
When I did my skydive,
I changed my attitude,
Afterwards I was in a far better mood.

I changed my diet and attitude,
And a positive way of health
and living with MS then ensued,
I changed my diet and stabilised, and recovered,
A new way of living I had discovered.

For 10 years from MS's claws I was released,
I found a kind of inner peace,
I took charge of MS,
I was in control, no longer a mess.

MS was stabilised, I stopped its progression,
And I came out of my depression,
I was no longer in an awful state,
I stabilised, recovered,
which was truly great.

That's when I met Steve,
now my husband, then my lover,
Now I'm not just a wife,
I'm also a mother,
A lot of the world together we discovered,
I'm so glad that I changed my attitude
and recovered.

Since 2009, the battle has resumed,
And by MS, at times I feel consumed,
I've had pneumonia, not once,
not twice, but thrice,
It's an understatement
to say it's not nice.

But I'm lucky, for 23 years
to have been alive,
It's truly remarkable that I've survived,
I've got MS,
That's Multiple Sclerosis.

I've also got Marcus and Steve,
Yes, I really do, indeed,
Marcus is my mini-Steve,
Something I find hard to believe.

I enjoy my time with my son,
And having with him, a lot of fun,
Marcus is 11 years old,
And, generally, is as good as gold.

With Steve, we're a family,
And Steve I still find very funny,
My Mum is SalFish,
But do not worry, my Mother, I do not diss.

She used to be called Miss Sally Fisher,
And good health for the rest of her life
I do wish her,
I was so happy the cancer was fixed,
I really love my Mum to bits.

She's Grandma with Marcus,
to me she's my Mum,
With her grandson, she has much fun,
Mum loves the composer Percy Grainger,
From her, he's far from a stranger.

In fact, he'd be her specialist subject
on Mastermind,
She says Percy was born way before his time,
Every time I hear my Mum's voice,
I'm so happy she's here and I rejoice!

The Meaning of Life
(aka John Shuttleworth should be Prime Minister)
(May 2018)

In many ways, this poem is the most difficult to explain, which poses the question: Is it the most me?

I don't know why or when I first got the idea of John Shuttleworth being Prime Minister but when I did, it struck me as being so ludicrous that actually he might make it work well.

Yes, I'm saying that despite John Shuttleworth being inept at quite a lot of things and not very good at most, he might actually be a good Prime Minister because at heart he is a good honest bloke, who just wants to do right by everyone.

I think he and we would muddle by, if he was Prime Minister.

The rest of the poem is about other questions my brain has asked. What's the meaning of life? Why are we here? Why so much inequality and unfairness in the world?

Serious questions, again I want to challenge people's thoughts a bit, but in a way that's weird, fun and, well, different.

And maybe I'm also trying to remind myself that even when faced with bad things in my life, it can be worse for others, plus that a good dose of humour helps me get through the day.

The Meaning of Life
aka
John Shuttleworth should be Prime Minister

I think John Shuttleworth should be
Prime Minister,
Maybe you think that sounds a bit sinister,
But I think he'd be really fair,
And that he really would care.

I don't think he'd be a tory,
But he'd restore Britain to its former glory,
He'd probably be more of a socialist,
And under him great policies would exist.

The Deputy Prime Minister
would be his agent, Ken,
They'd work in Parliament, by Big Ben,
His wife Mary is Minister of Shopping,
To him she delegates, Minister of Mopping.

So, what's the meaning of life?
I think it's to have fun,
But fun cannot be had by everyone,
For instance, in the Sudan,
A boy often doesn't live to become a man.

And if you're a girl,
It's an even tougher world,
Often, girls don't go to school,
They often don't go as a rule.

Some, on their 12th birthday they marry,
Getting pregnant before they miscarry,
Tragically, being a very young wife,
Damages their health and their life.

Kids walk miles for dirty water,
None comes from the taps, like it oughta,
Making them ill and too weak to cry,
Unfortunately, many of them simply die.

But maybe the meaning of life is sex,
Let me explain, you look perplexed,
Sex addiction is sweeping the nation,
Leading to lots of babies
through procreation.

Lots of babies means, many, many Kinder,
Whose disputes with parents,
are solved by Judge Rinder,
No, thinking again, the meaning of life is to have
fun,
When all is said and done.

If John Shuttleworth was Prime Minister,
if he won,
He'd definitely make life more fun,

If John was Prime Minister,
this is the thing,
He'd make us all his song to sing.

Two margarines on the go
That's how the singing would flow,
And all the pigeons would take flight,
Either in disgust or delight.

I tell you this secretly, between you and me,
John Shuttleworth for Prime Minister
it should be,
He'd solve all our problems from this day forth,
As fun solutions, our problems would dwarf.

Bladder Stone

The original idea behind doing a new poem came from my friend, Liz, who suggested that I give people a better idea of how my daily life is a battle from hour to hour, minute to minute, even down to the second to second of my life and what supports me in those hours, minutes and seconds, both good and bad.

When I came to do the poem, so much had gone on in the previous year that it came out as an update on my year of struggle for good health, and the additional obstacles I faced on top of a simple day in the life of Sylvia Wright. That wasn't the intention, but no poet can control the route of their creation when it takes on a mind of its own.

The poem does still shine a tiny light on how I cope with daily and ongoing life, my riddles and jokes and, through the help of my carers, so some of the original intent is there but subsumed within a greater different whole.

Bladder Stone
(March 2020)

A few years ago, I had a Bladder Stone,
Soon to over 5 cm, it had grown,
I did not want them to operate,
Because at the time my health wasn't great,
I didn't want another pneumonia bout,
Because with my health there was such doubt.

I could tell the doctors didn't want to operate,
So I left it alone and left it to fate,
The doctors felt I was too weak,
To put me to sleep,
They weren't sure I'd breathe again,
That I'd awaken to use my brain.

I decided against because the odds,
Better alive than with the gods,
Eventually that turned into a mistake,
That is the turn that fate did take,
For the Bladder Stone further from
5 cm had grown,
I really should not have left it alone.

In the end, leaving it was a mistake,
Because my catheters it continually did break,
The Stone was getting in the way,
And for that I did surely pay,
It caused my catheter to keep popping out,
The Bladder Stone had a lot of clout.

The catheters coming out was a real pain,
I had to look at the operation again,
They said I was far too weak to put to sleep,
Awake they said they would have me keep,
They said I could have an epidural in my spine,
And they hoped it would be fine.

I thought that without the operation
I would die,
For the following reasons is why,
The problem was my kidney
kept getting infections,
That was the conclusion of doctors
and inspections,

It was a serious threat, getting re-infected,
Especially when the urine got mis-directed.
It got stuck and couldn't come out
into the bladder,
All this made me sadder and sadder,

I thought without the operation I would die,
I didn't want it to be time to say goodbye,
I plucked up my courage,
Fortunately, I had some left in storage.

For I wanted the operation, risks and all,
So, this lady decided to lie tall,
I couldn't cope with the catheter
coming out every night,
Leaving me an awful and smelly sight,
Every morning covered in what I had pissed,
To have the operation was a necessary risk.

They did operate while I was awake,
But the anaesthetist lady was truly great,
I told her jokes and riddles
throughout the entire time,
And I came through without any water
and was fine,
Yes, I told her lots of jokes and riddles,
These made her laugh and have the giggles.

I went to hospital six times in six months,
Plenty more times than just the once,
Six months, six times and I survived,
I kept coming out somehow alive,
And then on top of it all I overdosed on water,
And in doing so myself I nearly slaughtered.

Because my sodium in my blood got too low,
I ended up in a coma for three days,
and didn't know,
I really had lost the plot,
Even over that I have got,
My life is still a daily struggle,
Through it, though, I still do muddle.

As I do, I can be a pain,
In my carers' lives I can be a bane,
But I've got great carers,
who are good to me,
And on the whole, I'm very happy,
I've had pneumonia and septicaemia
many times,
But somehow, I've always survived a
nd ended up fine.

I think all the time, I have to burp!
And it can drive my carers berserk,
But they are very loyal to me,
For that I am lucky, definitely.
My carers are called, Tiger,
Caroline, Yvonne and Claire,
They stay even though
I can be a nightmare.

Mum and Me Entwined Again

In the couple of years since I wrote the last poem about my Mum, she has developed a few memory problems. Mum tends to think of herself as a silly Sally because she knows her memory is not completely what it was. The rhyming of the word re-enforces that thought, I think.

I wanted to write the poem because I love my Mum and I wanted to reflect this, letting her know that this will always be the case, while still being honest about the problems she's facing.

When it came to write the poem, I was worried that I would over-emphasise Mum's problems and make them seem greater than they currently are. I don't think this happened in the end because of humour and the fact that I became entwined in the poem. As with my previous poem about my Mum, I ended up entwined in it unintentionally, but maybe that will always be the case for us.

My being entwined in the poem is good because it gave me something to compare Mum's problems with, namely me. It enabled me to show that they are not that bad as she has similar memory battles to me. Family and carers will confirm that my short-term memory is not what it was.

The outcome is a poem I am surprisingly pleased with.

Mum and Me Entwined Again
(March 2020)

My Mum is 79,
Until recently her fitness was fine,
Now she's got a problem with her
short-term memory,
For this, sadly, there's no remedy.

But my Mum shouldn't feel too blue,
Because she's got a son, called Matthew,
So actually, she has got a memory,
There is a *** remedy.

He looks after her all the time,
She needn't have too troubled a mind,
Even though she often feels confused,
And maybe even a little bemused.

She knows she's lucky to have such a son,
She's proud of him, that she's his Mum
So Mum may feel muddled,
But she really shouldn't feel troubled.

They live at The Fairway,
Where he looks after her night and day,
My mum calls herself Silly Sally,
While she lives above the Rivelin Valley.

But I don't agree that she's silly,
She just lives somewhere that is hilly,
She feels silly and stupid, but she isn't,
I'll prove it, now just listen.

Mum and me are the same,
Due to damage in our brain,
Maybe we feel silly and thick,
And think it's not nice living with this.

Maybe me and Mum feel a bit insane,
But we're not, we're just entwined again.

Steve Wright

I wrote this poem because of the impact of the disaster that was Steve's death. I know he's gone from my life, but I still don't want to believe it.

I guess the poem was the first real way I started processing the grief that naturally followed the passing of my husband, my sweetheart, on August 11th 2020.

On one level, I just needed to vent my emotion, my huge screaming loss.

Which is why the initial attempts at this poem were probably angrier than the final version.

Initially, I thought that the NHS had really messed up in failing to deal with a brain bleed he'd had and that it was their negligence that had killed him.

However, the final version reflects the fact that the coroner said he had died due to non-Hodgkin lymphoma, a cancer of the white blood cells.

That doesn't mean I still don't scream inside and wish they had picked it up early, when it was treatable, but as it isn't the easiest thing to diagnose, it makes my anger less.

The poem also fulfilled my need to have a contribution to his funeral service, to show what he meant to me as well as to process what he had gone through before his death. I can't say it was cathartic, but it fulfilled a need and was the stepping-stone I needed to get on with my life, to process the grief I felt then and still feel now.

I will always love you Steve, my husband, my sweetheart.

Ta-ta, Steve.

Steve Wright
(October 2020)

When I met Steve, it wasn't love
but laugh at first sight,
Being with him became a delight,
Through his actions he gave me the world,
Before me it, with him, unfurled.

We went many places
and many sights we did see,
Through his actions he made me very happy,
I was lucky to have 20 years of his life,
He made my life worth
all its trouble and strife.

That I would get better, he made me believe,
Because he was so sure and he was MY Steve,
I shared nearly 22 years of his life,
For 13 years of those, I was his wife.

I may originally have just been his lover,
But, most importantly, he made me a mother,
Steve was often like a god to me,
Because he looked after our family.

Steve went to the chiropractors,
who clicked his spine,
But the problems he had this didn't make fine,
Steve said there's really a lot more to this,
For a quick easy fix, is what I did wish.

As a scooter salesman he got a gold star,
He also enjoyed every classic American car,
Under a classic car, Steve banged his head,
Which caused a head injury, and it bled.

This itself didn't make him weak,
Steve also had pain in his cheek,
That sometimes came or went away,
But a lot of the time around it did stay.

When he couldn't properly lift his arms,
That's when I felt very alarmed,
I was really worried, I'm not lying,
It often sounded like he was dying.

Why Steve died, we didn't know the answer,
Then they told us it was cancer,
He had cancer in every white blood cell,
No wonder he felt really unwell.

Having had Steve as my husband, I was blessed,
At least he's no longer in pain, but at rest,
Marcus proved himself a real man
His Dad asked him for help, he said yes, I can.

Steve, in his life before this always did win,
His voice was fine
he could always whistle and sing,
He liked to laugh and loved a good joke,
He really was a truly good bloke.

For our house, his death is a disaster,
As we no longer have his laughter,
When Steve died, I felt really bereft,
Behind I never expected to be left.

Now I feel totally destroyed,
Like I've been hit by a meteoroid,
But Marcus, our son, will keep me going,
Love and support he's always showing.

We both have great memories of his Dad,
For those we will be forever glad,
We're glad in our lives Steve did exist,
A wonderful man who will be greatly missed.

Random Jokes
(Or are they riddles?)

1: A lady went to the doctors with a piece of lettuce poking out of her knickers, the doctor asked her why and she said "That's the tip of the iceberg."
(Peter Kay)

2: Yesterday, I started training for the Olympics and I feel great as I've only missed one day.

3: We asked a 100 undertakers if they wanted to be cremated, 99 said yes and one couldn't answer because he was having a cough-in fit.

4: On his 18th birthday, a man goes into a pub with his carer; this man has no body, just a head, and orders his first pint. He takes a first sip and suddenly his torso appears. He takes another sip and Hey Presto! his arms appear, he then takes a third sip and his legs and feet appear. He got really excited with this and started running all around the place, unfortunately then ran straight out into the road and was killed by a passing lorry. The bar tender was then heard to comment "That boy should have quit while he was ahead.".

5: A man wants to learn how to do the splits, so he contacts a man about training him. The man asks him, "How flexible are you?", he replies, "I can do next Tuesday.".

6: I like European food, so I decided to Russia over there, because I was Hungary, after Czeching the menu I ordered Turkey, when I was Finnished I told the waiter it's Spain good but there's Norway I could eat another bite.

7: Two aerials are talking, and one says to (asks) the other, "How was the wedding?". The other replies, "Oh the wedding was great but the reception was poor.".

8: There were two toadstools talking, and then one went on a date, she was then asked "How was the date?" She answers, "Oh, he was a fun guy." (fungi).

9: A man goes into a library and says, "Please can I have fish, chips, mushy peas and a battered sausage?". The librarian replies "But sir, this is a library.", he apologises and whispers, "Please can I have fish, chips, mushy peas and a battered sausage.".

10: A man says to a girl, "My mum says if I see a beautiful girl, I'll turn to stone, and you know what, I can feel myself getting hard already.".

11: A boy goes to school and says to his teacher, "Will I get told off for something I haven't done?". The teacher says, "Of course not, how can I tell you off for something you haven't done?". The boy replies, Good, I haven't done my homework, Miss.".

12: A wife is talking to her husband and she says, "You never put small amounts of money there.". He replies, no change there then.

13: A man complained after he got charged for a free satellite dish, he complained because the salesperson had told him it would be 'on the house'.

14: My friend went to Egypt and he saw a man covered in chocolate and sprinkled in nuts. It was the Pharaoh Rochette.

15: A man stole some rhubarb out of someone's garden; the police took him into custardy.

16: My sister-in-law had a vacuum cleaner, but she put it on eBay as it was just gathering dust.

17: The man from the chip shop went to prison; he got done for assault and battery.

18: I was going to tell you a joke about a sausage, but it was the Wurst.

19: There's a girl and a pizza. The pizza says to the girl, "What is the chemical formula for water?". The girl says, "hijklmno".The pizza says, "What are you talking about?" The girl replies, "Yesterday, you told me the chemical formula for water is $H2O$.".

20: There are two sketches in a race, it ended in a draw.

21: There were two very smartly dressed men in suits in another race, it ended in a tie.

22: A man's wife asked him for the Vaseline, he accidentaly gave her superglue. Surprisingly, he hasn't heard a word of criticism about his mistake.

23: Beethoven used to be a great composer, now he's just a decomposer.

24: A podiatrist's favourite animal is a toad.

25: A podiatrist's favourite food is toed in the hole.

26: When a podiatrist breaks down, they have to be towed.

27: We went to a zoo, it only had one dog in it, and it was a shit zoo.

28: If your freezer defrosts – don't make a meal of it!

29: We took the shell off a snail to see if it would go faster, but it just behaved sluggishly.

30: White sugars are very common, while brown sugars, demerara.

31: Chicken, its pretty fowl, isn't it?

32: Corn, it's just amaizeing!

33: There are two dragons in a race. What was the result of the race? It was a dead heat.

34: Santa's talking to his wife; he asks what the weather will be like; she replies, "It looks like reindeer."

35: A pony went into a bar but it could hardly speak, the barman asked, "Have you got a sore throat?". To which the pony replied, "No I'm just a little horse.".

36: The cheese was going to tell the Marmite a juvenile joke but decided that it was too mature to do so.

37: The man knew his bowling-alley job was short term as they said it was a tenpin (temping) position.

38: A mother called Susan was sitting down wearing an orange dress. We called her Satsuma.

39: A woman is starting to get tinnitus and complains about it to her husband. Later in the day, he comes in smiling and gives her some jewellery, she asks why, to which he replies, "You were talking about new earrings earlier dear.".

40: I was talking to my husband about making sure the safe was secure and he went out and bought jewellery. I think he heard me say lock it.

41: The male kitten was emotionally hurt whenever he went down a side street because he took everything purrsonalley.

42: There was a blonde policewoman, she was a fair cop. On her beat was an Avenue called Letsby, when arresting people there she always said "Let's be having you.".

44: The Knight who won the lottery was Sir Prized.

45: This lady wanted a telescope for her birthday, so her husband went to the shops to look into it.

46: I went to the shops to buy a six pack of Coke, but by mistake I picked 7 UP.

47: The woman, who was only half listening, stormed off when her husband asked her to put additional clothes on. She didn't like being called a more on.

48: There is a goat and she says to her husband, "I'm pregnant." Then she laughs and says, "Just kidding!".

Random Riddles
(Or are they jokes?)

Questions

Q1: What do you get if you cross a cow with a trampoline?

Q2: What Indian food is a canal boat?

Q3: What instrument doesn't like Joe?

Q4: What can you hold without touching it?

Q5: What gets wet the more it dries?

Q6: What spread could mum like?

Q7: What fruit preserve helps mum set the table?

Q8: What Michael Jackson song helps you make scrambled eggs?

Q9: What type of knowledge joins the army?

Q10: What three chocolate bars are out of this world?

Q11: What chocolate bar laughs?

Q12: Which box of chocolate runs a dating agency?

Q13: What chocolate bar talks very quietly?

Q14: What chocolate bar does ballet?

Q15: What chocolate bar makes little waves on a pond?

Q16: What chocolate bar is the subject of a conversation?

Q17: What chocolate bar can you only eat loudly?

Q18: What chocolate bar is a pirate's treasure?

Q19: What chocolate bar is milk, the fifth letter of the alphabet and the noise a sheep makes?

Q20: What biscuit enjoys going out at night?

Q21: Which biscuit waddles?

Q22: Which chocolate isn't yours?

Q23: What chocolate is like a wheel?

Q24: What chocolate bar is like a woman's permed hair?

Q25: What chocolate is very clever?

Q26: What biscuit is a tyre?

Q27: What tree is love sick?

Q28: Why did the snakes and ladders game start yawning?

Q29: What fish is a child's party dessert?

Q30: What fish is a Buddhist?

Q31: What fish is in the sky?

Q32: What fish sings in the right key?

Q33: What fish is always asleep?

Q34: What fish is always where it should be?

Q35: What fish is a pet?

Q36: What type of fish is out of breath?

Q37: What do you call a pen on a window ledge?

Q38: Why did the ruler not move?

Q39: What phone is always on the move?

Q40: What phone is in prison?

Q41: What herb is the end of the world when it runs out?

Q42: What are the most attractive fruits?

Q43: What's a man's favourite fruit?

Q44: What's a horse's favourite fruit?

Q45: What's a woman's favourite fruit?

Q46: What composer helps open a door?

Q47: Which two composers help you get the groceries?
Q48: Who's a dog's favourite composer?

Q49: Why is Donald Trump like a bird?

Q50: What's the most expensive meat?

Q51: Which are more expensive, birds or fishes?

Q52: What's the most expensive fish?

Q53: Which bank note sings opera?

Q54: Which coin is a police officer?

Q55: What always goes up and never down?

Q56: What has a head and tail but no body, or legs?

Q57: What precious vegetable is there 24 of, and is followed by a fruit?

Q58: Why did the taps go to bed?

Q59: Why was the baker so handsome?

Q60: Which vehicle did the players travel to the match with?

Q61: Where do roosters lay their eggs, in the north, south, east or west?

Q62: What coat can you only put on when wet?

Q63: What fish is on your foot?

Q64: Why is there no tea in China, some tea in a china pot and even more tea in a china teapot?

Q65: What fish goes on an ice rink?

Q66: What cheese is made backwards?

Q67: What cheese is how you milk a Welsh hedgehog?

Q68: How do you keep a duck's bill closed?

Q69: What berry is an OAP?

Q70: What nut do you flush down the toilet?

Q71: What nut keeps the house standing up?

Q72: What nut is a place in South America?

Q73: What nut is money and something you put on your foot?

Q74: What nut has chocolate in it?

Q75: What nut has flour in it?

Q76: What salad ingredient is the offer of an automobile and a female deer?

Q77: Which are richer, birds or fishes?

Q78: What nut is a vegetable?

Q79: What nut is brown?

Q80: What country is waiting for a bus?

Q81: What historic city is a ruler having a look?

Q82: Which country only ties one shoe lace?

Q83: In what city does the father help bring the shopping in?

Q84: In what country are people always smartly dressed?

Q85: In what country do female parents do very little?

Q86: What's the most dangerous musical instrument?

Q87: Why did the broken-down vehicle suddenly work when it was put on a ship?

Q88: What animal is a man playing golf?

Q89: Why was the hopping mammal's fur standing up?

Q90: What tree is when you bring it to the boil in balanced proportions?

Q91: Why did dog win the lottery?

Q92: What instrument helps fishermen fish?

Q93: Which country is a busker who is not rich?

Q94: Which city goes down the plughole to the devil?

Q95: What headache isn't yours?

Q96: Which tree is not me?

Q97: What fish is a rock?

Q98: What bird is a fish?

Q99: What bovine is a fish?

Q100: What tree rhymes?

Q101: What tree looks after people's teeth?

Q102: Whose boy was setting fire to things?

Q103: What tree is science?

Q104: Which Egyptian Pharaoh drives an automobile to la Luna while hitting the horn?

Q105: On which day of the week do you have an option?

Q106: Which car is good value and is like a pair of glasses?

Q107: What tree is in the kitchen?

Q108: What tree is a bedroom?

Q109: Where do you not want to read between the lines?

Q110: What clothing helps you apply for higher education?

Q111: What grain is anything?

Q112: What game is new-born babies and kisses?

Q113: What game is where you apologise a lot?

Q114: What game is what a surgeon does?

Q115: What game knocks you over a lot?

Q116: What goose is French?

Q117: Why did the girl who was given flowers have chapped lips?

Q118: What animal is only a cat?

Q119: What's a dog's favourite clothing?

Q120: If everyone in Britain owned a car, what flower would it be?

Q121: Which flower lives again and again and again?

Q122: Which flower is when a festive man sings, God Save the Queen, to his mother?

Q123: What do you call a three-legged donkey?

Q124: Why did the golfer wear two pairs of pants?

Q125: What did the police officer say to his stomach?

Q126: What's the difference between an Arsenal football player and Cinderella?

Q127: Why is there no aspirin in the jungle?

Q128: What's wooden and sticky?

Q129: What do you call a deer with no eyes?

Q130: What do you call a deer with no eyes and no legs?

Q131: What do you get if you eat too many Christmas decorations?

Q132: What do you call a dinosaur who's had a vindaloo?

Q133: What colour says "Come in"?

Q134: What animal makes the best teacher?

Q135: What do you call a male cow that falls asleep on you?

Q136: Why did the lobster blush?

Q137: Why did the tomato blush?

Q138: How do you spell 'potatoes'?

Q139: When's the best time to visit the dentist?

Q140: Why did the bull rush?

Q141: Why did the turtle cross the road?

Q142Where do you weigh a whale?

Q143: What is a poorly bird that breaks the law?

Q144: What do you call a camel with three humps?

Q145: What dinner service does a baby get in the womb?

Q146: Why do you call a bungalow a bungalow?

Q147: What do you call a pea that escapes from prison?

Q148: Why was 10 afraid of 7?

Q149: Why did the orange not want to take his skin off?

Q150: What do you call a man with no shins?

Q151: What do you call a man who loses his car?

Q152: How many tickles does it take to make an octopus laugh?

Q153: Why did the scarecrow win the Nobel Prize?

Q154: What did the big chimney say to the little chimney?

Q155: What do you call a woman, who has a pint of lager balanced on her head?

Q156: What do you call a woman in goal?

Q157: What do you call a woman, who is very, very tidy?

Q158: Why did the hen not get up until winter?

Q159: How did the scallop get into university?

Q160: Why did the skeleton go the party alone?

Q161: How do you put an elephant in a fridge?

Q162: How do you put a giraffe in a fridge?

Q163: If Simba held a meeting for all the animals, who would be last to the meeting?

Q164: If you come to a river that is known for its crocodiles, how do you get across?

Q165: How many elephants can you fit in a Mini?

Q166: How do you know if your mum has invited the elephants to a dinner party?

Q167: When swinging across the jungle, Tarzan looked up to the horizon and saw three elephants, what did he then say?

Q168: If Tarzan was swinging across the jungle and looked up to the horizon and saw three elephants with sunglasses on, what would he say?

Q169: What is the collective noun for zebras?

Q170: If there was a date for Star Wars Day, what would it be?

Q171: What do you eat on the beach?

Q172: What do you get when you cross a black magic woman and the seashore?

Q173: What did the orange say to the apple?

Q174: What do you call a pair of pears?

Q175: How many nuns could a nunchuk chuck if a nunchuck could chuck nuns?

Q176: Where does the general keep his armies?

Q177: Why do girls not go to Egypt?

Q178: Where do you find the meaning of life?

Q179: What's the difference between a jeweller and a jailer?

Q180: What did the accountant do when he got constipation?

Q181: What female name does the Tower of Pisa have?

Q182: What do you call a man with a car stuck to the back of his head?

Q183: What do you call a man with a car on his head?

Q184: What do you call a female pea?

Q185: What do you call a bean that goes on holiday outside the UK?

Q186: Why can Santa not get fired?

Q187: How many ears does Mr Spock have?

Q188: Why did the horse sneeze?

Q189: Why don't snails like takeaways?

Q190: Why did Santa have three gardens?

Q191: Why did Santa refuse to go down the chimney?

Q192: What's the most common owl in England?

Q193: Why did the maize start to laugh?

Q194: How did we know the humpback was upset?

Q195: How do we know the fishmonger was thinking only of himself?

Q196: How do you prepare for a party on Saturn?

Q197: Why did Santa's grotto have to close down?

Q198: Why is a house not like instant coffee?

Q199: Why did all the surgeons' patients laugh a lot?

Q200: Why do cows give milk not bulls?

Q201: Why did the cow hide in the corner?

Q202: Why was the bull hiding in the corner?

Q203: How does the gambler losing at chess win and pay off his losses?

Q204: Why did the man playing the violin go to prison?

Q205: Why did the patient go to prison?

Q206: What game do you play when the rubbish is collected?

Q207: Why was the builder frightened?

Q208: What do you call an eskimo's house with no toilet?

Q209: What did the butcher say when he shook hands?

Q210: What did the bus driver say to the frog?

Q211: What did the bus driver say to the frog? (new joke)

Q212: Which is the dirtiest toy?

Q213: What is a ton going forward and not coming back?

Q214: What tree is popular with the dead?

Q215: What tree is a dead person?

Q216: Why was Sherlock Holmes good at learning the Periodic Table?

Q217: Why is male kitten a human being?

Q218: Why did the male kitten down a back street take things to heart?

Q219: What sauce is very popular in cemeteries?

Q220: Which is the tallest building in town?

Q221: What composer says 'Hello Dennis'?

Q222: What food does Fireman Sam like best?

Q223: What was the vicar that died called?

Q224: How do we know that the stars in the sky are Conservatives?

Q225: Why does the woman say 'tarah' after getting a bargain?

Q226: What tool shagged the taxi man?

Q227: What instrument is an ice cream?

Q228: What vegetable is a police officer doing his rounds?

Q229: What vegetable is when you exclaim about a very fast plane?

Q230: Why do people sit around a birthday cake and sing?

Q231: Why was the electrician good at relationships?

Q232: Why do trees sigh heavily in the spring?

Q233: What letter is very strange?

Q234: What letter do you thank?

Q235: Which city is a very good cook, and a meadow?

Q236: Why did the architect have bad vision after designing and completing his latest building?

Q237: What two letters of the alphabet are very pretty?

Q238: What letters of the alphabet are very slow?

Q239: What capital city shows you the way to the sea?

Q240: Why didn't the movable steps feel like part of the family?

Q241: What bird works on a building site?

Q242: What adhesive do they use in prison?

Q243: What do you get when you cross a sheep and a kangaroo?

Q244: Where do trees come from?

Q245: Where do canines come from?

Q246: What tree grows corned beef?

Q247: What tree is at the end of your arms?

Q248: What tree grows next to the sea?

Q249: What tree is dressed like a wolf?

Q250: What did the bleach blond tree say to the other tree?

Q251: What did the bleach blond tree say when bugged about its roots showing?

Q252: Why do people with money like trees?

Q253: What did one tree say to another tree when it wouldn't get to the point?

Q254: Why do trees go to the doctor?

Q255: What did the tree say to his best mate?

Q256: What medical equipment does a tree climber use?

Q257: One tree was failing to understand what the other tree meant for ages, and then it suddenly understood. What did it say?

Q258: What wood do you find in a bathroom?

Q259: Why did the man from the lemonade factory run away?

Q260: What does a bus taste of?

Q261: Why was the ketchup flirting?

Q262: Why was the baguette kept in a cage at the zoo?

Q263: What Lake protects a woman very well?

Q264: Which doctor is very lazy?

Q265: A man keeps proposing to people. What's his name?

Q266: Which male name is a lie?
a. (Clue: the first Christmas Carol?)

Q267: Which is a male name that tells the truth?
b. (Clue: the Ark)

Q268: What female clothing is where you live?

Riddle Answers

A1: Milkshake

A2: An (onion) bhaji

A3: A banjo

A4: Your breath (or a conversation)

A5: A towel

A6: Marmite

A7: Marmalade

A8: Beat it

A9: General knowledge

A10: Mars, Galaxy and Milky Way

A11: Snickers (Sniggers)

A12: Matchmakers

A13: A Wispa

A14: A Twirl

A15: A Ripple

A16: A Topic

A17: A Crunchie

A18: A Bounty

A19: A Milky Baaaaa

A20: A Club biscuit

A21: A Penguin

A22: Terry's (Chocolate Orange)

A23: A Rolo

A24: A Curly Whirly

A25: Smarties

A26: A Wagon Wheel

A27: A Sycamore (sick amour)

A28: Because it was a board (bored) game

A29: A jellyfish

A30: A monkfish

A31: A starfish

A32: An in-tuna fish

A33: A kipper

A34: A (in)plaice

A35: A catfish

A36: A puffer fish

A37: A pencil

A38: Because it was stationary

A39: A mobile phone

A40: A cell phone

A41: Thyme

A42: Bananas, they're very appealing

A43: Men always like a nice pear

A44: A strawberry

A45: Mango

A46: Handel

A47: Chopin, Liszt

A48: Bach

A49: Because he tweets a lot

A50: Deer

A51: Birds are cheaper

A52: A goldfish

A53: A tenor

A54: A copper

A55: Your age

A56: A coin

A57: 24 carrot golden delicious

A58: Because they were drained

A59: Because he was well bred

A60: Their coach

A61: None of these, they don't lay eggs as roosters are male!

A62: A coat of paint

A63: A sole fish

A64: Look at the number of ts in the words

A65: A skate

A66: Edam

A67: Caerphilly

A68: Using duc(k)t-tape

A69: An elderberry

A70: A peanut

A71: A walnut

A72: A Brazil nut

A73: A cashew nut

A74: A coconut

A75: A doughnut

A76: An avocado(e)

A77: Fishes, they have the river banks

A78: A peanut

A79: A hazelnut.

A80: Kuwait

A81: Peking

A82: Taiwan

A83: Baghdad

A84: Thailand

A85: Malaysia

A86: A nukulele

A87: Because it was cargo

A88: Manatee

A89: Because the situation was hare raising!

A90: Symmetry

A91: Because it ate Winalot

A92: Castanets

A93: Singapore.

A94: Helsinki

A95: Migraine

A96: A yew tree

A97: A stonefish

A98: A parrotfish

A99: A cowfish

A100: Poetry

A101: Dentistry

A102: Arson

A103: Chemistry

A104: Tutankhamun

A105: Tuesday

A106: A Ford Focus

A107: A pantry

A108: A dormitory

A109: On a train track

A110: A uniform

A111: Go one, give me the answer, tell me oat!

A112: Noughts and crosses

A113: Sorry

A114: Operation

A115: (Ten pin) bowling

A116: The mongoose

A117: Because she was given tulips

A118: A meerkat

A119: Pant

A120: Carnation

A121: Reincarnation

A122: Chrysanthemum

A123: A wonkey

A124: In case he got a hole in one

A125: You under a vest

A126: Cinderella gets to the ball

A127: Because the parrots-eat-em-all

A128: A stick

A129: No idea

A130: Still no idea

A131: Tinselitus

A132: A mega-sore-arse

A133: In-digo

A134: A tort-oise(us)

A135: A bulldozer

A136: Because the sea weed

A137: Because it saw the salad dressing

A138: OOOOOOOO (put 8 Os)

A139: Too,th,urty

A140: Because it saw the cowslip

A141: To get to the get to the Shell station

A142: At the railway (whale weigh) station

A143: An ill eagle (illegal)

A144: Humphry

A145: Womb (room) service

A146: Because they bung a low roof on it

A147: An escapee

A148: Because 7, 8, 9 and 10 was next

A149: Because it didn't appeal to him

A150: Tony

A151: Carlos

A152: Ten tickles (tentacles)

A153: For being outstanding in his field!

A154: You're too young to be smoking

A155: Beatrice (beer tricks)

A156: Annette

A157: Anita

A158: Because she was no spring chicken

A159: She won a scallopship

A160: Because it had no body to go with

A161: Open the door put it in, close the door

A162: Open the door, take the elephant out, put it in, and close the door.

A163: The giraffe, as he's still in the fridge?

A164: Easily, you swim, as all the crocodiles are at the meeting

A165: 5, 3 in the back and 2 in the front

A166: They'll be a Mini parked out front!

A167: Oh look, three elephants

A168: He would say nothing, as he wouldn't recognise them

A169: A crossing

A170: May the forth

A171: A sandwich

A172: A sand witch

A173: You look fruity

A174: A pair

A175: Nun

A176: Up his sleavies

A177: Because they come back as mummies!

A178: In a dictionary!

A179: One sells watches and the other watches cells

A180: He sat down and worked it out with a pencil

A181: Eileen

A182: Reg

A183: Jack

A184: A chick pea

A185: Abroad bean

A186: Because he's already got the sack (and it's keeping him in work)

A187: Three, the left ear, the right ear and the final front ear

A188: Because it had hay fever

A189: Because it's fast food

A190: So he could ho, ho, ho

A191: Because he was claustrophobic

A192: A tea t'owl

A193: Because it told a very corny joke
Wheat a minute, did he say it with a wry smile?
I barley know how to answer that.

A194: Because we could hear it wailing and blubbering

A195: Because he was very shellfish when he came to sell fish

A196: You planet

A197: For elf and safety reasons

A198: Because it's a proper tea

A199: Because he had them in stitches

A200: Because bulls charge

A201: Because it was being bullied

A202: Because it was a coward.

A203: By cheque mate

A204: Because he was on the fiddle

A205: Because after the operation, the surgeon stitched him up

A206: Bin-go

A207: Because he was bricking it

A208: An Ig

A209: Nice to meat you

A210: Hop on

A211: You can't get on, toaday

A212: The toilet

A213: Not

A214: A cemetery

A215: An ash tree

A216: It was elementary, dear Watson

A217: Because he's a purrson

A218: Because he took everything purrsonalley

A219: Gravy

A220: The library, it has many stories

A221: Hyden

A222: Samphire

A223: Pastor way

A224: We saw them from the observatory

A225: Because it was a good buy

A226: The screwdriver

A227: A cornet

A228: Beetroot

A229: Courgette

A230: Because it's covered in icing

A231: Because he was down to earth and there was always a good connection and a spark

A232: Because it's when they are re-leaved

A233: A weird O

A234: (Thank) Q

A235: Sheffield

A236: Because it was an eyesore

A237: QT

A238: A Q

A239: Beirut

A240: Because they were a step ladder

A241: A crane

A242: Sellotape

A243: A woolly jumper

A244: Barking

A245: The Isle of Dogs

A246: A 'corn beef' ash tree

A247: A palm tree

A248: A beach tree

A249: A fir tree

A250: Oh my god. my roots are showing

A251: Oh leaf me alone

A252: They have branches in every town

A253: Stop beating around the bush

A254: For treatment

A255: Hey Bud

A256: Ivy

A257: I've just twigged what you mean

A258: Toiletries

A259: Because he bottled it

A260: Chocolate, it's a Double Decker

A261: Because it was feeling saucy

A262: Because it was bread in captivity

A263: Lake Garda

A264: Doctor Doolittle

A265: Neil

A266: Noel (there is an L in it)

A267: Noah (There isn't an R in it)

A268: A dress

Random Thoughts and Facts
Weird, Random and Wise?

(Stupid sayings (in my opinion))

1: Saying NO COMMENT, well that is a comment, hello!

2: Saying, I'm SPEECHLESS, no you're not, you're saying something.

3: If you are talking to someone and you say "I'm not arguing", well hello that is an argument or at least the start of one.

4: If I were you, I would do this, no not true, if I were you, I would do what you do, this is different from what I'd do in your position, but that's not what people say.

Stupid mis-sayings (by me)

1: "Can you get pneumonia from getting air in your lungs?" I meant moist air.

Thoughts

1: Funny thing from faith, God is sexist, and I think I might agree because in churches you don't sing hers you sing hymns, and when you say a prayer, at the end of the prayer you don't say awomen, you say amen. And, also, do you know what God's name is? His name is Peter, because at the end of the prayer they say thanks be to (Pete(r)) God.

2: When my uncle was a kid he used to think it was called not Marks & Spencer's but Marks Expensive. He also used to think it was called not C&A but See & Pay.

3: It's funny that when you ring someone up you can get the engaged tone, because you also give someone a ring when you get engaged to them.

4: Which came first, the name for a disposable hanky, a tissue, or the supposed sound for a sneeze, atishoo?

5: Why is it called a fine, when you don't feel fine when you get one?

6: Why when you say, "It's freezing.", do people say "Tell me about it.", when you just did?

7: They say money doesn't grow on trees, but I disagree, as apples do, and you get pounds and pounds of them on a tree.

8: You know windows, when they get broken, they can be a right pain.

9:Why do we say "What on Earth's the matter?", when the Earth is the matter?

10: It's funny that funerals start with fun.

11: Why do people run to Sheffield when they have to leave home in a hurry? It's because it's an anagram of 'If She Fled' and 'If He's Fled'

12: A pane of glass likes winning the lottery because it's win dough time.

13: Funny how the word 'mental' starts with men! (Men reply, that's because women drive us there!)

14: Before people get married, they get engaged, before people get divorced, they get enraged. The only difference is the letters 'grrrr'.

15: Why do people say oops-a-daisy? You can't trip over a daisy.

16: You know garbage, litter etc.? Oh ignore me, I'm just talking rubbish, sorry for being rude and trash talking.

17: When you promise to get married, you get engaged. When you lock the toilet door, it says engaged. By doing so are you promising to marry the toilet?

18: A joke to play on people, ask them to say toast 20 times and then ask them what you put in a toaster, often they will say toast, when it's actually bread.

19: If a car goes on a plane, does it become cargo?

20: If you're asked if you're going somewhere today, don't answer, 'yes terday', as that's in the past and is impossible.

21: I used to go to church now and then, but I never went religiously.

22: I'm very clever; I know this because the word genius has both I and US in it.

23: The beach and the sea are talking: Sea: I see, but are you sure? Beach: Yes, I'm sure.

24: The letter U says to another letter, "You're a weird O". The letter O replies, "No, I'm not, you are, as you're an O with no top to it.".

25: Why are chilli peppers so hot when they sound so cold?

26: Steve, my husband, was often both mum and dad so he was either MAD or DUM or perhaps he was just a MADUM.

27: Lawyers: their cases are often lawsuits. Put them together and you get suitcases. Suitcases can be both open and shut. Lawyers' suits are often open and shut cases.

28: The reason I'll live forever is because my inability to walk means I can never be on my last legs and whenever I try and kick the bucket I miss.

29: Why, at dinner time, do parents tell kids to finish their plates? I mean do they want them to eat the plate too?

30: I'm confused as to why the word for mother in English is Mum and in German it is Mutter. I mean, are they silent or not?

31: I've worked out why you can't say bad things about a woman's clothes, it's because is causes dis-dress (distress).
32: Hospitals having sick bays is a basic requirement.

33: There no letters in the alphabet because:
A B flew away
CD were off playing music
E F'd off with F
G whizzed off
H2O is water
P is flushed down the toilet
The Q got on the bus
R and S were RSted
T has been eaten
UV is light, we can't see
W, two ewes have run away
X has exited
Y has disappeared, we don't know why
Z is asleep, zzzzzzzz.

34: I suppose we should be unsurprised that bakers have to have a brain to make bread and turn a profit. After all, you need a brain to knead dough before you can make any dough.

Ideas for T-shirts and Cards

1: A card that says Happy Anniversimas day or Happy Annibirthmas time.

2: T-shirts for men saying: I'm the woman of this house.

3: T-shirts for women saying: I'm the man of this house.

-

Random fact

How many knees does a spider have? 48.

The Ruder and Un-PC Section.

Wise or unwise?

(It's humour!)

No offence intended. Enter and enjoy.

Random Jokes (or are they riddles)

1: Three Irish blokes turn up for a job, the bloke advertising the job asks, "How long have you been lumberjacks?" They say, "What you talkin' about? We're not lumberjacks, the advert just said you wanted t'ree fellas.".

2: I was talking to a friend the other day and he said, I used to be a serial killer, but I can't get the packets open any more.

3: A woman is in the bath and there's a knock at the door, she says, "Who is it?", "The blind man", he replies. She says, "Come in." He enters and says, "Nice tits, where do you want me to hang the blinds?".

4: A boy goes up to his dad and asks, "What's a c**t?", his dad replies, "It's another word for a vagina". So his son then asks, "What's a vagina?", his dad replies "Oh you'll learn when you get older, it's something very special.". The boy ponders this and then replies, "Well mummy thinks you're very special.".

5: A husband asked his wife why she never told him when she was about to orgasm; she replied "But you don't like me ringing you at work?"

6: A girl goes home to her parents and says, "Mother, I'm pregnant", the Mother replies "Ah but are you sure it's yours?".

7: A_bloke goes to North America and he visits a Native American village. While he's visiting this village, one of the tribesmen tells him that he must go and see the All-knowledgeable One, who is really impressive. So he says, "Right I will do" and they usher him down to a tepee at the end of the village. They go in and they tell him to ask the All-knowledgeable One any question he likes and he will answer it.

So, he thinks, I'll get him and asks who won the World Cup in 1966. The old Native American looks up at him and says, "England in front of 96,446 fans, 15 people died that day, three were involved in accidents. The rest missed the game because of transport or other reasons." The bloke leaves very impressed.
30 years later, he goes back with his new wife, and he wants to impress her. Once at the village, he asks if the All-knowledgeable One is still alive and, of course,

the All-knowledgeable One is still there, so he takes his wife down to the see him.

He introduces her politely and, as he has great respect for the All-knowledgeable One, he greets him by saying, "How".

To which the All-knowledgeable One replies "Last-minute goal by Geoff Hurst".

8: Three nuns are killed in an accident and go up to heaven and they see St Peter at the Gate and he says I've got a question for each of you; you'll get into heaven if you get it right.

Question 1 to the first nun, "What was the name of Eve's partner?" She answers "Adam", St Peter says "Yes, that's right" and lets her in.

Question 2 to the second nun, "What was the name of the garden in which they met"? She answers, "The Garden of Eden.", St Peter says "That's right." and lets her in.

Question 3 was to the third nun, who was the Mother Superior, so, St Peter says, "This will be a bit more difficult. What did Eve say to Adam when they first met?" The Mother Superior is puzzled, scratches her head and says, "Ooh this is a hard one." St Peter says, "That's right." and lets her in.

Random Riddles Xtra

Q1: What vegetable is a dad who's had a vasectomy?

Q2: What are a man's three favourite birds?

Q3: What tree is a vagina?

Q4: What's the definition of masturbation? (Peter Kay)

Q5: Why did the Mexican push his wife off a cliff?

Q6: What's the difference between a tractor and a giraffe?

Q7: Two topless women drive past a large expanse of water. What's it called?

Random Riddles Xtra Answers

A1: A parsnip

A2: Two great tits and a swallow

A3: A country

A4: A waste of f***ing time!

A5: Tequila

A6: One has hydraulics and the other has high bollocks

A7: Lake Titicaca

Thoughts

1: You know women get the menopause, does this mean they pause the men or do they not let men get their paws on them?

2: We all know that when you drink tea it turns into pee, but why are only Native Americans honest enough to acknowledge it? Why don't we all call our houses teepees?

3: You shouldn't swear, it's not classy, although it can be useful to emphasise a point. Oh, that reminds me, I should thank you for reading my fucking book!

Sylvie Wright 2022

That's
All
Folks!

(But Not Quite. PTO.)

Books in the Cybermouse Range
by
Bill Allerton;

The Fox & The Fish   (ISBN: 978-0-9548373-2-7)

Firelight on Dark Water   (ISBN: 978-0-9548373-2-7)

A Day for Tigers   (ISBN: 978-0-9930424-3-0)

Magpie   (ISBN: 978-0-9930424-5-4)

Watch & Wait   (ISBN: 978-0-9548373-1-0)

Childrens Fiction:

Foxes, Frogs & Rice Pudding (ISBN: 978-0-9930424-6-1)

Sir Tingly & The Quest for The Dargon

(ISBN: 978-0-9548373-7-2)

The Time Mouse   (He's running late...)

Podcasts;

Urban Tiger Radio (For Adults)

Urban Tiger Radio Childrens Hour

(Search Amazon for 'Bill Allerton')